TOWARD STEWARDSHIP

TOWARD STEWARDSHIP

An Interim Ethic of Poverty, Power and Pollution

by
William J. Byron, S.J.

PAULIST PRESS
New York / Paramus / Toronto

Library of Congress
Catalog Card Number: 74-30806

ISBN: 0-8091-1865-3

Published by Paulist Press
Editorial Office: 1865 Broadway, N.Y., N.Y. 10023
Business Office: 400 Sette Drive, Paramus, N.J. 07652

Printed and bound in the
United States of America

Contents

53300

Contents

Editor's Foreword

I chided my esteemed co-editor for the modesty of his proposed title, "An *Interim* Ethic." My suggestion was to drop the italics and keep the rest. I had two reasons for so suggesting. First, he has achieved a noteworthy synthesis of the Judao-Christian tradition as found in the Bible and other historical sources with the economics of development, a subject in which he has done considerable research. The result bids fair to stay on the social ethics register for some time to come. It will not remain unchallenged, hopefully, in this era of ethical pluralism but it will hold its own.

Second, the professional ethicist has reached the stage of expanded consciousness where he accepts the pilgrim's staff and cloak as the symbols of his trade. In the search for moral truth on the highway of ongoing history he regularly stops off to check the map. "Here we are at the moment," he says, "and here's where we're going," though he knows full well there are alternate routes. There are other maps as well. Every ethic is interim. That's because ethics is a reflection on life and life no longer stands still, as we find to our discomfort. There can no longer be one route, one map journeys.

Fr. Byron does not take the stance of suspended motion, as the economist turned social ethicist well might, so complex are the economic and ethical factors he

grapples with. He has heeded the criticism John Court-
ney Murray directed some years ago of "ambiguism"
against social ethicists who found the international
scene too complex and ambiguous for ethics to render
judgment upon.

Take his treatment of the oppressed poor. Fr.
Byron refuses to let us off by the escapist route of "the
poor you have always with you" or some other biblical
oversimplification. His theme of stewardship rings
through and through with accountability. We are all ac-
countable to others now living and the future generations of humankind, before God, of the use we make of
the earth's resources. We may not take refuge either in
the institution of private ownership we still cling to.
However well that ethical model served in an earlier
age it is no longer viable. Read the author's thesis of
the economic empowerment of the poor and see why.

Where do the poor get the power to improve their
lot? The answer to this ethical whodunit lies in the economic analysis of power. I refuse to give away his de-
nouement. Suffice it to say that the word "power" had
been consigned to the hell of bad words. Reinhold Nie-
buhr, a giant among social ethicists of our time, did
that quite successfully with his *Moral Man, Immoral
Society*. We lesser figures had become aware of (I al-
most said sick of) its dastardly and bullying use in politics both domestically and between nations. But the
politics of power and the economics thereof are two different things though related. Personally I never thought
until recently that we would polish up the tarnished old
word and bring it out of hell, redeemed for recycled
use.

It is not just in the empowerment of the poor (un-
derdeveloped) that Fr. Byron advances ethical ar-

gument. He is to be credited with breaking new ground also in his development of social sin and his treatment of the ecology question. How we can and ought to finance our efforts to clear the air and unmuddy our water—I mean literally, not metaphorically—he says forthrightly.

Robert H. Springer
Woodstock College, New York

Introduction

John the Baptizer, in preparing "the way of the Lord," expounded an ethic that is outlined in the Gospel of Luke. "The crowds asked John, 'What ought we to do?' " They were seeking ethical advice.

In reply he said, "Let the man with two coats give to him who has none. The man who has food should do the same." Tax collectors also came to be baptized, and they said to him, "Teacher, what are we to do?" He answered them, "Exact nothing over and above your fixed amount." Soldiers likewise asked him, "What about us?" He told them, "Do not bully anyone. Denounce no one falsely. Be content with your pay" (Lk. 3:10-14).

"Using exhortations of this sort," says Luke, John "preached the good news to the people."

Contemporary Americans would not unanimously agree that such radical instruction is necessarily good news. Many would prefer not to include such Gospel principles with the propositions to which they give their Christian creedal assent. They remember another Gospel assertion, "You have the poor with you always" (a line which a religious educator friend of mine believes would surely head some celestial list of remarks Jesus wishes he hadn't said!) and use it, with self-persuasive misinterpretation, to avoid the egalitarian conclusions repeatedly proclaimed in the New Testament.

Yet, in preparing us for Christ, John announced a spare-and-share ethic that has never caught on but won't die out. This book attempts to deal with that ethic in the vocabulary of stewardship and in the context of poverty, power and environmental pollution. It is an interim ethic in this sense: it guides us on that long, long way toward the ideal of a Christian community set forth in the Acts of the Apostles:

The faithful all lived together and owned everything in common; they sold their goods and possessions and shared out the proceeds among themselves according to what each one needed. They went as a body to the temple every day but met in their houses for the breaking of bread; they shared their goods gladly and generously; they praised God and were looked up to by everyone. Day by day the Lord added to their community those destined to be saved (Acts 2:44-47).

This is really a description of the Church—that community assembled around the belief that Jesus is Lord and the Father raised him from the dead, a community which preserves in its midst the virtues of faith, hope and love, and which remembers its Lord in the breaking of the bread.[1]

Through the centuries of the Christian era, that Church has had to deal with shifting cultures and evolving social orders. John the Baptizer paved the way of the Lord with radical doctrine, but did not, apparently, regard the destruction of the political and economic system as prerequisite to the establishment of that doctrine. He spoke of consumer behavior (sharing) within the system. He acknowledged a proper role for tax collectors, but insisted that they do their job justly. Even soldiers had a place, but exploitation and unjust accusation did not. And to advise someone to "be content with your pay" implies at least a minimal acceptance of some inequality in the economic order. Relative, not absolute, egalitarianism would appear to be consistent with the ethic John is proposing. It would be difficult, in any case, to imagine him opposing a reduction in inequality.

Perhaps John never thought in terms of systems. Perhaps, if he were around today, he would offer a radical critique of Western capitalism's tendency to produce both poverty and pollution as by-products of technological advance, and recommend the dismantling of the system. I doubt that he would take a conservative stance, praising the free-enterprise system and insisting that less government would provide improved social welfare. (He did, after all, line up on the side of the tax collectors, so long as they acted justly.) I would hope that he wouldn't absolutize any system as good or bad, but profess something of a contemporary liberal faith that, original sin and organizational complexity notwithstanding, representative governments can guide economic systems toward the best possible balance of four values which conservatives and liberals alike hold dear: freedom, equality, social order and social justice. The conservative is willing to live with inequality if it is necessary to guarantee maximum freedom; he will also tolerate some social injustice as a price for continuing social order. The liberal will have fewer qualms about upsetting the social order to gain more social justice; he will yield on freedom to enhance equality. The contemporary radical thinks that none of the four values will be achievable for long within a capitalist system that requires greedy acquisition and self-interested competition for its own survival. If man is to survive, that system must be destroyed; so runs the radical critique.[2] So, in my mind, arises the need for an interim ethic.

The argument of this book will reflect a liberal bias, a Christian commitment and an economic approach to the solution of social problems. All three elements fit under the rubric of social ethics. Only the letters immediately preceding the last punctuation mark on the final page of this book constitute the last word. Nowhere in these pages is a final statement offered that purports to solve our problems of poverty and pollution.

The argument and the ethic carry us "toward" stewardship. A brief first chapter will touch upon the notion of stewardship. Then chapters two and three will develop the major argument of the book—theological reflections on the economic problems of poverty and environmental pollution. A final chapter will ponder the question of whether Christ really consigned the poor to be always with us.

A Dano Frodan cartoon in the *New Yorker* had one sherry-sipping plutocrat remark to another, "If God hadn't wanted there to be poor people, he would have made us rich people more generous."[3] The argument of this book rests on the assumption that he made us more generous than we want to admit. What is needed is a new awareness of our responsibility to do what we are perfectly capable of doing—to share the things we hold in trust.

NOTES

1. Conversations with William V. Dych, S.J. provided me with this simple description and profound definition of the Church of Christ.

2. For an introduction to these categories and an exposition of the radical critique, see David M. Gordon (ed.), *Problems in Political Economy* (Boston: D. C. Heath, 1971). For a very brief and readable contemporary statement of the liberal belief "that a gradual reduction in inequality and expansion of equality of opportunity is both desirable and feasible," see Paul A. Samuelson, "Inequality," *Newsweek*, December 17, 1973, p. 84.

3. *New Yorker*, November 12, 1973, p. 114.

1. The Idea of Stewardship

"Idea" is a word pronounced differently in various parts of the United States. Southern EYE-dehs are qualitatively comparable to i-DEAHs elsewhere in the country. But as any schoolboy in any part of the nation knows, when his mother inserts a "very" for emphasis, and breaks the word into three distinct syllables with the accent in the middle, his proposal is not likely to see the light of day.

The idea of stewardship has been around for quite a while. Contemporary Catholics tend to regard it as a Protestant concept unrelated to the core of their Catholic commitment. Many Protestants tend to associate stewardship with support of the church and with pastoral accountability for the use of funds. Whatever their initial reaction to the word, all too many affluent American Christians, when confronted with the challenge of a biblically-based notion of stewardship, raise their eyebrows, close their checkbooks and mumble: "The very i-DE-ah!"

Wealth possessed is held in trust for others. This is the fundamental idea of stewardship. The possession of wealth involves, therefore, serious social responsibilities. The greater the wealth, the more awesome the responsibility.

11

Chapter 25 of the Book of Leviticus opens with Yahweh speaking to Moses on Mount Sinai and instructing him to "speak to the sons of Israel and say to them: 'When you enter the land that I am giving you. . . .' " There follows a set of guidelines on the use of land. The first set of instructions concludes with the words: "You must put my laws and customs into practice; you must keep them, practice them; and so you shall be secure in your possession of the land. The land will give its fruit, you will eat your fill and live in security" (Lv. 25:18-19).

Central to this exposition of man's relationship to the land is the affirmation that "the land belongs to me, and to me you are only strangers and guests" (Lv. 25:23). Accordingly, the psalmist provides, throughout the 39th Psalm, an appropriate and prayerful response for man, the guest, to God, the owner—the Lord.

Each man that stands on earth is only a puff of wind,
every man that walks, only a shadow,
and the wealth he amasses is only a puff of wind—
he does not know who will take it next. . . .
Yahweh, hear my prayer;
listen to my cry for help,
do not stay deaf to my crying.
I am your guest, and only for a time,
a nomad like all my ancestors.
Look away, let me draw breath,
before I go away and am no more!
(Ps. 39:6-7, 12-13)

The idea of stewardship catches this guest relationship that characterizes man-on-the-land entrusted with wealth that belongs to God. We own nothing absolutely; we are stewards. And, as St. Paul remarks, "What is expected of stewards is that each one should be found worthy of his trust" (1 Cor. 4:2).

John the Evangelist examines the "worthiness" of the steward not in juridical terms but from the perspective of love: "If a man that was rich enough in this world's goods saw that one of his brothers was in need, but closed his heart to him, how could the love of God be living in him?" (1 Jn. 3:17). And in the very next verse St. John gently prods the Christian on to action: "Our love is not to be just words or mere talk, but something real and active."

Ideas need legs. How does the idea of stewardship become both real and active in the Christian community? Perhaps a somewhat self-interested response to the "energy crisis" might mark a beginning of a revival of the notion of stewardship in America.

Just as the Earth is finite, so also are its food, land, water and air. The Earth is like a spaceship journeying in Venus with a limited supply of life-supporting resources. In the interest of our own survival and that of our offspring, we must *exercise a wise stewardship* over its resources. Events of recent years have made us increasingly aware of this very fundamental obligation and of how it is ignored.[1]

As I write, American motorists are fighting long lines, short tempers and one another as they search for their share of a short supply of gasoline. Whether the shortage is genuine or contrived, it signals a possible future change in American lifestyle. Perhaps we will become more sparing and sharing. Perhaps we will be less mobile. Perhaps our streets will become cleaner, our air purer, and our weekends more domestic. But of greater significance, I think, is the challenge the current energy crisis places before the Christian to make a positive, manifold response to the question stewardship constantly asks: Do I share enough? The energy crisis could be moving us toward stewardship. But we had better move fully and fast; otherwise we will be faced with an embarrassing instance of the world evangelizing the Church!

At the international level, a no-growth solution to our energy and environmental problems is unacceptable. Too many people have too much growing to do economically to be content with a steady-state economy designed to cut pollution in the wealthy nations and also conserve non-renewable resources for eventual consumption in rich lands. Hence the need to change the composition of growth in the rich economies (fewer jet trails but more nursing care, for example), and at the same time shift capital and technology to the poor lands where hard economic growth can occur, thus generating both wealth and income to be shared by people moving up from poverty.

Christian stewardship will have to be outward-looking and dynamic, not stingy and static. Wise stewardship will mean the application of creative intellect to all our problems, including the multiple problem of discovering alternative sources of energy, avoiding any deleterious ecological effects of such discoveries, and making such advances economically available to the poor nations.

If, for instance, the stewardship (read, "wise use") of ideas leads to the economically practicable development of solar energy, why—since the sun shines on rich lands and poor—should this not benefit the poor nations? Only if the necessary technology, embodied in the necessary capital, is denied them. Only, in other words, if the rich do not share enough. But land, sea, sun and air are given by God for the use of all. The idea of stewardship would, it seems, suggest that solar energy be extended to all who can benefit by it and who need it.

Reflection on the stewardship of ideas might prompt one to recall that Jesus used his parable of the talents to praise outward-looking and dynamic stewardship, and to blame the stingy and static. His argument is based on the assumption that our resources are not ours absolutely, but only held in trust. Included in our wealth of resources are not just the non-renewable ones but also human intellect and imagination. Christian stewardship calls for dedicated application of intellect and imagination to human problems. Perhaps this truly missionary force will be released by the energy crisis.

There is a serious moral obligation involved in all of this. Barbara Ward, famous economist, author and consultant to both the Vatican and the United Nations, saw it in these terms:

The majority of Christians live in the developed North and if this area is wealthy far beyond the general level of world society, they (the Christians) profit from this unbalanced prosperity and must in conscience account for their stewardship.[2]

American Catholics, the most affluent in the world, need a good deal of help arriving at the stage where they can see the issue in terms of a conscience problem. The American free enterprise system does, after all, rest (at least theoretically) on the institution of private property. But Catholic theology has had a lot to say about free enterprise. Much of this has been said in papal encyclicals and other documents of the teaching Church. Subsequent chapters of this book will highlight some of that teaching. Later discussion will also show that the longest Catholic-Christian theological tradition understands the *use* of property to be common (and this by divine plan), while the *ownership* of property *may* be private (as the best accommodation to the fallen state of sinful man).

Where free enterprise exists, the freedom of the enterpriser is limited, not absolute. The limits come from the societal implications contained in the idea of stewardship: wealth possessed is held in trust for others.

The right to own private property is not absolute. Freedom of use of private property is not absolute. What then of the right to accumulate property—how much? What is the moral limit on the right to pass property on to one's own heirs or beneficiaries of one's own choosing? Theology can give no more precise answer to these and related questions than St. Peter gave when he wrote:

Above all, never let your love for each other grow insincere, since "love covers over many a sin." Welcome each other into your houses without grumbling. Each of you has received a special grace, so, like good stewards responsible for all these different graces of God, put yourselves at the service of others (1 Pet. 4:8-11).

To share "without grumbling" seems to be the demand that the idea of stewardship is placing upon the contemporary Catholic. The sharing may be through higher taxes so that income can be redistributed in favor of the poor, or higher prices so that poor laborers can be more justly compensated for their efforts in putting products—coffee, tea, bananas, grapes, lettuce or whatever—on the rich nation's table. Many other forms of sharing are also called for.

An encouraging, positive indication that this spirit of sharing may be surfacing in America appeared in

1974 in connection with the annual "Super Sunday" ritual which brings an estimated 70-million televiewers into an electronic community-experience as they witness professional football's annual Super Bowl. The Associated Press reported this significant development as follows:

Fran Tarkenton, quarterback of the Minnesota Vikings, has donated his $7,500 share of the Vikings' Super Bowl earnings to funds for the ailing and the handicapped.

Tarkenton told the Minneapolis Star he made the decision prior to the Super Bowl to give half of his earnings to Daytop Village, a drug rehabilitation program in New York, and half to the Minneapolis Association for Retarded Children.

He said, "The game has been good to me financially. Sometimes I feel a little awkward when I meet and talk with people who need. I mean, I look at my own life and say, 'It's exciting and good and prosperous.' Then I remember all the noble words about trying to ease the hardships of others. All of us try to help some time or other. But I think a person always has to ask himself: 'Do I share enough of myself?' "[3]

At issue, of course, is how many people among the thousands in the stadium or the millions witnessing the Super Bowl on television would agree with Quarterback Tarkenton. If most of the participants, spectators and beneficiaries of Super Sunday shared Fran Tarkenton's viewpoint, then it might be suggested that the idea of stewardship is alive and well in Christian America. But such is not the case. To communicate one quarterback's attitude to 70 million fans is *the* pastoral challenge for the American Church today.

William J. Keech's brief book, *The Life I Owe*,[4] is subtitled, "Christian Stewardship as a Way of Life." Keech draws wisely and heavily from a 1959 paper by Union Theological Seminary Professor James Smart, "The Theological Groundwork for Christian Stewardship Education."[5] Dr. Smart's "groundwork" deserves selective retracing:

There is no surer test of the character of our faith in God than how we deal with what we consider belongs to us. To believe in God as our Creator and in Jesus Christ as our Lord and to yield ourselves to the rule of God as he comes to possess us in his Spirit is to acknowledge that we are not our own, nor is there anything that is primarily ours. . . . And my possessions, though I have earned them all by my own labor, are not mine. If for a moment I delude myself into thinking they are mine, I hear a voice saying, "Thou fool, this night shall thy soul be required of thee. Then whose shall these things be that thou has provided?"[6]

America received a terrible jolt when its economy all but collapsed in the early 1930's. A perceptive novelist of that period, Thomas Wolfe, was able to see the existence then of a spiritual problem that appears to be with us again. An economic crisis disclosed that problem in the 1930's. Watergate and the energy crisis are revealing it once again in the 1970's. Professor Smart suggested that our grasp of the idea of stewardship is the surest "test of the character of our faith in God." When significant numbers of its citizens fail that test, a Christian nation is in very deep trouble. Thomas Wolfe saw the failure this way:

What happened in Libya Hill and elsewhere has been described in the learned tomes of the overnight economists as a breakdown of "the system, the capitalist system." Yes, it was that. But it was also much more than that. In Libya Hill it was the total disintegration of what, in so many different ways, the lives of all these people had come to be. It went much deeper than the mere obliteration of bank accounts, the extinction of paper profits, and the loss of property. It was the ruin of men who found out, as soon as these symbols of their outward success had been destroyed, that they had nothing left—no inner equivalent from which they might now draw new strength. It was the ruin of men who, discovering not only that their values were false but that they had never had any substance whatsoever, now saw at last the emptiness and hollowness of their lives. Therefore they killed themselves; and those who did not die by their own hands died by the knowledge that they were already dead.[7]

St. Luke records a parable of Jesus which contains a one-word summary-description of the man Wolfe portrayed: Fool. "But God said to him, 'Fool! This very night the demand will be made for your soul; and this hoard of yours, whose will it be then?' So it is when a man stores up treasure for himself in place of making himself rich in the sight of God" (Lk. 12:20-21). A Christian drift from stewardship to selfishness is just plain foolishness. Such a drift, as more of Wolfe's prose movingly suggests, can weaken the very fabric of a nation:

Sometimes it seems to me . . . that America went off the track somewhere—back around the time of the Civil War, or pretty soon afterwards. Instead of going ahead and developing along the line in which the country started out, it got shunted off in another direction—and now we look around and see we've gone places we didn't mean to go. Suddenly we realize that America has turned into something ugly—and vicious —and corroded at the heart of its power with easy wealth and graft and special privilege. . . . And the worst of it is the intellectual dishonesty which all of this corruption has bred. People are *afraid* to think straight —*afraid* to face themselves—*afraid* to look at things and see them as they are. We've become like a nation of advertising men, all hiding behind catch phrases like "prosperity" and "rugged individualism" and "the American way." And the real things like freedom, and equal opportunity, and the integrity and worth of the individual—things that have belonged to the American dream since the beginning—they have become just words, too. The substance has gone out of them— they're not real anymore.[8]

Behind our scrambled response to the energy crisis, behind our uneasiness with pressures for an improved distribution of wealth and income in America and around the world, behind our hesitation about equality, stands a problem of faith. Too few of us really believe that the dominion is God's, and that we own nothing absolutely. Too few of us regard ourselves as stewards of wealth, seriously obliged to use it for the good of others. Too few of us have the courage to look at the data of revelation that touch upon these matters and conclude that our salvation literally depends on our willingness to take the Lord God seriously when he declares himself as owner and us as guests. In consequence of our failure in this regard, too few of us are willing to pay up so that many of our society's problems can be put down. If Pogo was perceptive in saying to Porky that we are "at the crossroads of the past, present and future," his comic-strip companion was even more perceptive and refreshingly practical when he replied, "Where's the toll booth?"

Part of the toll American Christians should certainly be willing to pay, here at the crossroads of the future, is an expenditure of intellectual effort to understand *theologically* the problems of poverty, pollution and the scarcity of resources. Theology is, after all, an exercise of understanding. As the next two chapters will suggest, social science is a congenial partner for theology, and contemporary problems call for serious reflection in the light of revelation. Much of that reflection remains to be done.

But understanding, whether theological or socially scientific, is not enough. Action must follow. And as the Christian citizen moves down the action road, the toll collection will be real. If the idea of stewardship ever gets legs, progress will come about only to the extent that those in possession of property, power and prestige (elements which the author of *The Affluent Society*[9] calls the "three basic benefits from wealth") are willing to let go.

NOTES

1. Joseph M. Moran, Michael D. Morgan and James H. Wiersma, *An Introduction to Environmental Sciences* (Boston: Little, Brown and Company, 1973); quoted by R. W. Behan, "The Liturgy of the Environment," *Worldview* (January, 1974), p. 29. Emphasis added.

2. Quoted by George H. Dunne, S.J., *The Right to Development* (New York: Paulist Press, 1974), ch. 3.

3. *Saint Louis Globe Democrat*, January 16, 1974.

4. Valley Forge: The Judson Press, 1963.

5. An Address at the Workshop on Christian Stewardship Education, Buck Hill Falls, Pa., March 1959 (New York: Department of Stewardship Education, National Council of Churches of Christ in the U.S.A.).

6. Quoted in Keech, *op. cit.*, p. 19.

7. *You Can't Go Home Again* (New York: Harper, 1934), pp. 369-370.

8. *Ibid.*, p. 393.

9. John Kenneth Galbraith, *The Affluent Society* (Boston: Houghton-Mifflin, 1958), p. 88.

2. The Economic Empowerment of the Poor

A Theological Reflection

The task of theology in the Church today is to articulate the relationship between Christian faith and contemporary experience. Theology must therefore be in touch with non-theological disciplines—notably the social sciences—for an accurate reading and competent analysis of contemporary experience. Practical or pastoral theology, also informed by the social sciences, must be alert to identify and examine in the light of the Gospel the ways in which men live the Christian faith in the contemporary world. Since the practice of life (and therefore of faith) is impeded by a variety of contemporary problems, theological reflection, if it is to be integral, relevant and thus self-justifying, must be particularly sensitive to the problems that impede the full development of human potential. One such problem is involuntary, oppressive poverty.

My effort here will be to elaborate a theological argument for the economic empowerment of the poor. I understand poverty to be sustained deprivation, and economic poverty to be sustained deprivation of income and wealth (and, derivatively, deprivation of health, shelter, food, education, employment and human dignity to the extent that this last derives from all the rest). I understand power to be the ability to cause or prevent change.

In reflecting theologically on the link-up of these elements (poverty, wealth, income and power), I propose to begin with a reference to current data, followed by a brief sketch of the development of the argument through scriptural, patristic, medieval and conciliar sources, as well as to contemporary theological opinion.

First the data. Who has the wealth in America? By wealth is meant personal property and financial assets. Income—the flow of dollars received in a given period —is something quite distinct. The distribution of income is uneven in America, but the nation's wealth is even more unequally shared. Citing "the best available current estimate," supplied by James D. Smith of Pennsylvania State University, *Business Week* reports that the top one percent of adult American wealth-holders own twenty-five percent or more of all personal property and financial assets.[1] Roughly 1.5 million people own one trillion dollars of the nation's wealth. The University of Michigan's Survey Research Center estimates that the wealthiest five percent of American families hold more than 40 percent of the nation's wealth.

Redistribution of wealth in favor of the poor could be attempted within our system chiefly by reform measures related to inheritance (death) taxes, and to some extent by reform of our tax policies with respect to money made by the sale of property and financial assets (capital gains). An equal distribution, desirable not only for the benefits it would deliver to those who now hold no wealth, but also because it would broaden

53300

the political base of our present economic system, is not likely to be achieved by the tax reforms just suggested. An equal distribution achieved in some other way, say, by expropriation, would, in my judgment, have worse social effects than exist in the present dispensation. Redistribution of *income*, through income tax reform, is, I think, a much more hopeful route.

There is a chicken-and-egg relationship between income and wealth. High incomes generate savings. Out of accumulated savings, property and financial assets are acquired; thus wealth is born. From this wealth, further income is derived.

Reform of the personal and corporate income tax, on the one side, coupled with an increase in public transfer payments (e.g., a federally financed income maintenance program) on the other, could have a signiificant redistributive effect on the nation's income. There are forces opposed to this redistributive shift, but identification of these forces must await our discussion of power.

For now, let these statements simply stand in place as data for reflection:

With equal distribution, each 10 percent of the population would get 10 percent of all income; each 10 percent would own 10 percent of total wealth.

But in fact, the top 10 percent of the American population gets 29 percent of annual income from wages, salaries, rents, dividends and interest, while these same top 10 percent *own* 56 percent of the wealth (personal property and financial assets).

The bottom 10 percent of the people get one percent of our income; they are, moreover, negative wealth holders, i.e., they owe more than they own.[2]

These data, it should be noted, refer only to wealth and income distribution in the United States. International comparisons between this, the wealthiest of all nations, and the poor of the world reveal a yawning gap that continues to widen.

The fact that we Americans, constituting as we do 6 percent of the world's population, consume or control 40 percent of the world's resources is a statistical commonplace. The social, political and moral implications of this statistic are better understood with the help of a simple metaphor. Imagine the world's resources to be a flowing river with all the inhabitants of the earth lining its banks. The flow is adequate to meet the needs of all the tribes along the banks. One tribe, representing 6 percent of the population of all tribes, finds itself in a privileged position upstream. By a mixture of craft and cunning, deceit and drive, it has succeeded in diverting 40 percent of the flow to serve its own tribal purposes. This small tribe's gain is taken at the expense of the impoverished majority downstream. Is it any wonder that not everyone who stands along those banks has an affectionate regard for the privileged 6 percent? The river metaphor is not a recent invention. "For thus says the Lord, 'I will spread prosperity over her like a river' " (Is. 66:12).[3]

International comparisons of wealth (or the lack thereof) cannot be made with any precision. The best indicator we have is a figure we call per-capita income. This is calculated by taking the Gross National Product (the market price-tag on all new goods and services produced in a given country in a given year) and placing that figure in the numerator, and then taking the national population figure for a denominator. But this index is by no means distortion-proof. If, for instance, a GNP of $1000 is spread over a population of 10, the per-capita income would be $100 in the extreme maldistribution situation where $991 of the income derived from the sale of this annual product went to only one man, while the other nine received no more than a dollar each. The per-capita figure would also be $100 if the income were divided equally over the total population of ten. Per-capita income figures tell us a lot for purposes of international comparisons, but they tell us nothing about the distribution of income within a nation.

Per-capita income for the United States is over $5,000 currently, as compared with about $150 for Bolivia, $60 for Ethiopia, $70 for Haiti, $80 for India, and $90 for Indonesia. These data should supply an adequate response to the question, "Who has the wealth?"

Next, I would raise the question: Does wealth equal power? Here opinion and fact must necessarily intertwine. Certainly, wealth can effect or prevent change, so wealth is powerful. Yet wealth is protected by law; hence law might be even more powerful. Is money power? In some circumstances, yes. But again, the power of money income is relative. I believe that power resides in a combination of three factors: numbers, resources and organization.[4] In the United States the numbers and resources are with the middle class, but there is no organization. America's poor have significant numbers (about one-fifth of the nation), but their resources remain unknown to themselves (particularly their personal and spiritual resources) and they, too, are unorganized. The rich have the financial resources, quite obviously. (They also have resources of intellect, health, culture and contacts, and some at least are spiritually conditioned to make it through the "eye of the needle.") The rich are relatively few in number and therefore vulnerable. They have organization to the extent that their status is reinforced by the dominant values of our society, and also to the extent that wealth and income are protected by law. The law, however, is changeable; so are dominant social values.

Small wealthy elites do have power, of course, but mainly because they seize opportunities or fill vacuums created by larger masses of less resourceful, unorganized persons. It is my view that poverty exists in America because the middle class does not have the will to eliminate it through a change in law and a shift in dominant values. Why not? Because the chance to own property and accumulate wealth is the dominant social motivation of participants in the American economic system. Those who hold the property and the wealth enjoy the privileges associated with them. But those who aspire to more property and wealth, and to higher incomes as a means toward these ends, are seeking the same privileges and do not want to see them disappear from the "American way of life." Such aspirations are so commonplace as to practically characterize the middle class.

Where then is power in America? In my view, it resides in strongest potential, if not in actual exercise, with the middle class. I therefore look to the middle class as the enabling force for the empowerment of the poor at home and, less immediately, but no less really, for the empowerment of the poor abroad.[5] Put it this way: In the War on Poverty, who is on the other side? I would reply: The middle class.

On a wall in the New York headquarters of Catholic Relief Services, the overseas aid division of the U.S. Catholic Conference, hangs a poster which reads:

"They say the poor have it hard. Well, the hardest thing they have is us!" A mental conversion of the last word into two initials and a shift of vision to a global context makes one wonder about U.S. efforts to ease poverty in the less economically developed parts of the world. As an American student remarked to me upon his return from a visit to several Third World countries, "U.S. Foreign Aid is a program designed to transfer funds from the poor people of a rich nation to the rich people of a poor nation." Not a fully informed opinion, of course, but not altogether wide of the mark either.

Poverty, as I indicated earlier, is sustained deprivation. Deprived of what? Sustained by what or by whom? What poverty involves for the impoverished is familiar enough conceptually, if not experientially, to permit us to move directly to the question: "Sustained by what, or by whom?" It is precisely here that the issues of oppressive social structures and possible social sin enter the argument. These must be part of any theological reflection on poverty. Such considerations are finding their way slowly into print in the recent literature on the theology of development and the theology of liberation. I shall touch upon social structures and social sin after first referring briefly to scriptural, patristic and conciliar expressions of a doctrine which would encourage the economic empowerment of the poor today.

Scripture

My guide here is James P. M. Walsh, S.J. whose unpublished paper "Scripture and Poverty"[6] lightly but expertly recapitulates the development of the notion of poverty in biblical tradition.

The eighth chapter of the First Book of Samuel gives the reader an idea of how monarchic Israelite society worked. Prior to the establishment of a monarchy, Israel was "relatively egalitarian," according to Walsh, who goes on to say that "from the late tenth century on, a minority became rich and the majority of the people were dispossessed of their inheritance in Israel, and the poverty of the many was a function of the new wealth of the few, and this process represented a real change in the traditions of Israel."

In the eighth chapter of the First Book of Samuel, we read that the "elders of Israel" come to Samuel, their judge (a technical term for a charismatic leader called by God to deliver his people from their pagan oppressors) and prophet, and asked Samuel to "give us a king, to rule over us like the other nations" (1 Sam. 8:5). *The Jerusalem Bible* footnotes this verse with the comment: "Israel forgets that it is not like other nations; in following their example and casting off Yahweh, its true king, it denies its special vocation."

In any case, Samuel responds to this request with a hostile description of the institution of monarchy; his response constitutes a warning:[7]

These will be the rights of the king who is to reign over you. He will take your sons and assign them to his chariotry and cavalry, and they will run in front of his chariot. He will use them as leaders of a thousand and leaders of fifty; he will make them plow his plowland and harvest his harvest and make his weapons of war and the gear for his chariots. He will also take your daughters as perfumers, cooks and bakers. He will take the best of your fields, of your vineyards and olive groves and give them to his officials. He will take the best of your maidservants, of your cattle and your donkeys, and make them work for him. He will tithe your flocks, and you yourselves will become his slaves. When that day comes, you will cry out on account of the king you have chosen for yourselves, but on that day God will not answer you (1 Sam. 8:11-18).

The author who puts this description on the lips of Samuel is drawing from an experience of monarchy that was unknown until the days of Solomon. The point of quoting the description is "because it gives us some sense of how monarchic Israelite society worked, and because it obviously presupposes an antecedent state of affairs—the happy condition of being free—that the author considers to be somehow more authentically Israelite."[8]

This change from relative egalitarianism to a condition where some are rich at the expense of the poor represents a departure from tradition and is therefore regarded as infidelity. Hence, the prophets denounce the rich not because they happen to have possessions, but because their actions violate covenant traditions.

Fr. Walsh offers an array of texts to support his thesis—for instance, Isaiah 1:21-26:

What a harlot she has become,
the faithful city, Zion, that was all justice!
Once integrity lived there,
but now assassins. . . .
All are greedy for profit
and chase after bribes.
They show no justice to the orphan,
the cause of the widow is never heard.
Therefore—it is the Lord Yahweh Sabaoth who speaks,
the Mighty One of Israel—
'I will turn my hand against you,
I will smelt away your dross in the furnace,
I will remove all your base metal from you.

I will restore your judges as of old,
your counselors as in bygone days.
Then you will be called
City of Integrity, Faithful City.'

As the language here suggests, greed and injustice
in property matters amount to harlotry, the familiar
biblical metaphor for cultic infidelity. The psalmist asserts that "the grasping man blasphemes" and "spurns
Yahweh" (Ps. 10:3).

The prophet Amos calls attention to "what great
disorder there is in that city (Israel), what oppression is
found inside her. They know nothing of fair dealing—it
is Yahweh who speaks—they cram their palaces full by
harshness and extortion" (Am. 3:9-10). The prophet
then announces Yahweh's declaration that an enemy
will invade the country, its power will be destroyed, its
palaces looted (Am. 3:11). Israel's exploitative behavior, constituting as it does infidelity, serves only to
"hasten the reign of violence" (Am. 6:3). Isaiah warns
that trouble is in store for those "who refuse justice to
the unfortunate and cheat the poor among my people of
their rights" (Is. 10:2). And again, "Woe to those who
for a bribe acquit the guilty and cheat the good man of
his due" (Is. 5:23). Those guilty of this kind of oppression will be punished "for rejecting the law of Yahweh
Sabaoth, and despising the word of the Holy One of
Israel" (Is. 5:24).

The point which Fr. Walsh makes with the support
of these and other texts is that there is a rejection of the
law embodied in imperial Israel's exploitation of the
poor. The exploitation brings forth oracles of doom.
The "rich" became identified with the "wicked" in both
the Psalter and the prophetic writings. "The identification," says Walsh, "proceeds from the very sound in-

sight that wealth derives from other people, whom the process transforms into the poor." The poor man is assured in the Psalter and by the prophets that divine justice will vindicate him. "The presupposition of this assurance is the hard-headed realization that the poor man is poor precisely because he refuses to play by the rich man's rules, because he keeps the law of the Lord. Hence the familiar identification in biblical tradition of the poor man and the just man."[10] The poor remain faithful to the covenant and to the Israelite tradition of relative egalitarianism and sharing. In sum, and in simplicity, the poor man is the just man.

Moving now into the New Testament, it is interesting to see how the Letter of James excoriates the rich for having "condemned, even killed, the just man":

You rich, weep and wail over your impending miseries. Your wealth has rotted, your fine wardrobe has grown moth-eaten, your gold and silver have corroded, and their corrosion shall be a testimony against you; it will devour your flesh like a fire. See what you have stored up for yourselves against the last days. Here, crying aloud, are the wages you withheld from the farmhands who harvested your fields. The shouts of the harvesters have reached the ears of the Lord of hosts. You lived in wanton luxury on the earth; you fattened yourselves for the day of slaughter. You condemned, even killed, the just man; he does not resist you (Jas. 5:1-6).

An untouched surplus, piled up in un- or mal-distributed heaps, is evidence of injustice. It is accumulated at the expense of the poor who are just, not because they are poor, but because their poverty is a result of their refusal to play the plunderer's role. There is something essentially Christian about "letting go," "pouring out," "giving up," "going without," "hanging loose," "sharing all" and, in consequence of this open-handed stance, "being free." At bottom, biblical poverty, whether in its Old or New Testament exposition, is a personal attitude.

"Have this attitude in you which was also in Christ Jesus" (Phil. 2:5); have this mind-set, this worldview that Paul attributes to the historical Jesus:

Who though of divine status,
did not treat like a miser's booty
his right to be like God,
but emptied himself of it,
to take up the status of a slave.[11]

Again, in the Corinthian correspondence Paul writes: "Remember how generous the Lord Jesus was: he was rich, but he became poor for your sake, to make you rich out of his poverty" (2 Cor. 8:9).

The self-emptying of Christ, his "kenotic" stance praised in the Christological hymn of Philippians 2:6-11, is the paradigm for Christian poverty. Commenting on this text, James Walsh says that Jesus "thus reveals God as the one who did not cling, the one who 'lets go.' "[12] The Philippians text really says it all. Additional texts could be discussed, but the point has already been made. The first beatitude, the renunciation texts in Luke, the detachment texts in Mark, the "social gospel" of Matthew 25, the exhortation in James 2:1-7 that social preference accorded to the rich over the poor is inconsistent with faith in Jesus Christ—all these and the many more that could be cited underscore a continuity of Old and New Testaments in identifying the poor man as the just man. Moreover, they spell out for the Christian the implications of the application of that Old Testament poor-equals-just-man typology to

Christ. The true Christian, therefore, not only sees his Master in the poor, but walks with an awareness that he wanders from the following of Christ if he is unwilling to "let go" so that others might benefit from his poverty. The heightening of this awareness is an urgent task for Christian moral education today. The goal, of course, of all living and learning that derives from these biblical insights is a Christian world where no one is rich and no one is destitute, but all are decently poor.[13]

What comes through to me, therefore, from this scriptural reflection on wealth and poverty is this: contemporary man should exercise his fidelity toward God by restructuring institutional arrangements that distribute wealth, income and power to one at the expense of another. Perfect egalitarianism is not the objective, but a social order free of exploitative economic relationships is.

Patristic Insights

My favorite text from the Church Fathers on wealth and poverty is in St. Basil's *Homily on Avarice:*

So you are not a miser, nor do you rob, yet you treat as your own what you have received in trust for others! Do we not say that the man who steals the coat of another is a thief? And what other name does he deserve who, being able to clothe the naked, yet refuses? The bread you keep belongs to the hungry; the clothes you store away belong to the naked; the shoes that moulder in your closets belong to those that have none; the money you have buried belongs to the needy. Therefore, you have wronged all those to whom you could have given and did not.

This is very strong and direct language, typical of

the beautiful bluntness of the early Church Fathers.

Another sample of patristic teaching on wealth and poverty would be Cyprian's mention of sharing with the poor in the context of reparative penance. In *De Lapsis*, No. 11, there is an interesting parallel to the Old Testament denunciations of the rich as unfaithful. Cyprian condemns riches as enemies of the faith. His people did not flee the persecution of Decius, he says, because they were too attached to their possessions:

What deceived many was a blind attachment to their patrimony, and if they were not free and ready to take themselves away, it was because their property held them in chains. That is what fettered those who remained, those were the chains which shackled their courage and choked their faith and hampered their judgment and throttled their souls, so that the serpent, whom God had condemned to eat of earth, found in them his food and his prey, because they clung to the things of earth.

Again, the blunt language about the non-alliance with wealth. I think it best to simply let the early Christian writers speak for themselves. What follows is only a sampling, but the message is clear. One is tempted to say "clear and unavoidable," but centuries of Christian history demonstrate that conclusions in favor of the poor have been systematically avoided in countries that call themselves Christian. At any rate, here are some words of St. John Chrysostom (*Homily 11*, on Luke 16:19-31):

The rich are in possession of the goods of the poor, even if they have acquired them honestly or inherited them legally.

When we refuse to give alms and to share, we deserve

to be punished as thieves. We are just as much at fault as those tax collectors who divert everyone's money to their own needs.

The wealthy are a species of the bandit.

And from Chrysostom's sixth homily on the Epistle to Titus, chapter two:

Asceticism benefits the ascetic, but does not save anyone else. Almsgiving profits all. It is the mother of charity . . . which is preferred to miracles and covers all sins.

Finally, in his comments on Matthew's Gospel, Homily 50, John Chrysostom makes a point that is seldom heard in modern pulpits:

God never condemned anyone for not enriching our temples with magnificent furniture, but he threatens with hell those who do not give alms.

Lest the texts multiply and bound upward on the scale of idealism, let me conclude this very random selection of early Christian writing with a line from Clement of Alexandria's thoughts on *The Rich Man's Salvation*, Chapter 13: "What society could exist on earth, if no one owned anything?" Some private property is necessary. Some accumulation will necessarily result. Some provision must be made for the future. One's own immediate needs and those of his family do have prior claim. Hence the need for an interim ethic, a spirit and a direction as we not only own and use property but move, with the help of divine grace, toward the Christian communitarian ideal.

Medieval Theologians

Rene Laurentin notes that it is in their teaching and development of the biblical doctrine on land that the Fathers of the Church addressed themselves unequivocally to the issue of wealth.[14] The land, symbol of the goods of the earth, belongs to God and is given equally to all. No man owns exclusively what is only his to share. The medieval theologians did not, according to Laurentin, dispute the patristic doctrine that by natural right all goods are common to all men. They did, however, make the distinction that explains common ownership as suitable had not man inherited original sin, and private ownership as suitable to sinful man. The experience of each of us does verify that we care more for personal than community property.

Urgent need, however, justifies the poor man's exercise of his fundamental right in considering as common those goods which will meet his necessity but which happen now to be privately owned. Laurentin points out that the following adage was a universally accepted thesis in the Middle Ages: "He who takes what is necessary does not commit theft, but takes possession of what is his own" (*Non committit furtum, sed suum accipit*).[15] As Laurentin explains, it was up to the 16th century commonly taught by the Church that "the common purpose for all goods is prior to appropriation. The right of private property is a secondary human right, destined to facilitate the proper use of goods."[16]

This doctrine was eventually obscured under pressure of 18th- and 19th-century economic liberalism—a term not to be confused with contemporary economic liberalism. The original economic liberals were those who wanted men and markets to be totally free of any kind of government regulation—free to maximize their own interests, profits and personal satisfactions. The economic liberal, forerunner of today's conservative, believed that somehow the unfettered play of market forces would generate the best achievable level of social welfare. In any case, Laurentin indicates that Cajetan's 16th-century misinterpretation of St. Thomas Aquinas prepared the way theologically for the displacement of traditional Church doctrine on property (common use is the primary right, private ownership secondary) by the rising liberal ideology. "Two successive articles on the *Summa Theologica*, II-II (q. 66, aa. 1 and 2), explain the common purpose of goods which is primary and fundamental, and then the individual appropriation which intervenes on a secondary level as a means of guaranteeing the proper management of wealth. Cajetan interpreted as private property what St. Thomas called common purpose. Thus private property was conceived as primary and of divine right."[17]

Although not every theologian followed Cajetan down the wrong path, the enthronement of the right to private property was not widely questioned. When the late 19th- and early 20th-century collectivist assault on modern capitalism emerged, the teaching Church overreacted. In underscoring its denunciation of the atheist ideology in Marxist "theology," the magisterium put its weight solidly behind the right to private property. In doing so, the Church not only encouraged unsophisticated believers to practically absolutize private property rights, but also missed some principles of Marxist economics which are perfectly consistent with Christian doctrine.[18]

The sequence of the Church's traditional teaching

on the question of wealth should be noted: common purpose is primary, private ownership is secondary. If you wish, put it this way: use is common; ownership may be private in order to facilitate the common use. A reversal of both traditional emphasis and traditional intent appears in late 19th- and early 20th-century theological reflection. The right to private property becomes primary and, in the understanding of many, absolute. The common use becomes something of an exhortatory guideline or moral restraint to be noted by the private owner in the exercise of his presumptively absolute right.

Second Vatican Council

Rene Laurentin quotes from the first schema prepared by the doctrinal commission of Vatican II to show how the exaltation of private property "as a primary, divine, and in some sense absolute right" bid for inclusion in the document which was to become the *Pastoral Constitution on the Church in the Modern World (Gaudium et Spes).*[18] The final text, accepted and promulgated as official conciliar teaching, is quite different. The interested reader may want to follow my footnote references to Laurentin's study which quotes generously from the original draft document. For our present purposes, however, I shall quote below only from the final document which was promulgated by the Council Fathers on December 7, 1965, one day before the closing of the Council:

God intended the earth and all that it contains for the use of every human being and people. Thus, as all men follow justice and unite in charity, created goods should abound for them on a reasonable basis. Whatever the forms of ownership may be, as adapted to the legitimate institutions of people according to diverse and changeable circumstances, attention must always be paid to the universal purpose for which created goods are meant. In using them, therefore, a man should regard his lawful possessions not merely as his own but also as common property in the sense that they should accrue to the benefit of not only himself but of others.

For the rest, the right to have a share of earthly goods sufficient for oneself and one's family belongs to everyone. The Fathers and Doctors of the Church held this view, teaching that men are obliged to come to the relief of the poor, and to do so not merely out of their superfluous goods. If a person is in extreme necessity, he has the right to take from the riches of others what he himself needs. Since there are so many people in this world afflicted with hunger, this sacred Council urges all, both individuals and governments, to remember the saying of the Fathers: "Feed the man dying of hunger, because if you have not fed him you have killed him." (Cf. Gratian, *Decretum*, C. 21, dist. LXXXVI, Friedberg I, 302; see also PL 54, 591 A.) According to their ability, let all individuals and governments undertake a genuine sharing of their goods. Let them use these goods especially to provide individuals and nations with the means for helping and developing themselves (*Gaudium et Spes*, n. 69).

Ownership and other forms of private control over material goods contribute to the expression of personality. . . .

Private ownership or some other kind of dominion over material goods provides everyone with a wholly necessary area of independence, and should be regarded as an extension of human freedom. . . .

The right of private control, however, is not opposed to

the right inherent in various forms of public ownership. Still, goods can be transferred to the public domain only by the competent authority, according to the demands and within the limits of the common good, and with fair compensation. It is a further right of public authority to guard against any misuse of private property which injures the common good.

By its very nature, private property has a social quality deriving from the law of the communal purpose of earthly goods (*Gaudium et Spes*, n. 71).

Less than two years after the Council, on March 26, 1967, Pope Paul VI issued his famous enclyclical *Populorum Progressio (On the Development of Peoples)*. The short section on property is given here in full:

"If someone who has the riches of this world sees his brother in need and closes his heart to him, how does the love of God abide in him?" (1 Jn. 3:17). It is well known how strong were the words used by the Fathers of the Church to describe the proper attitude of persons who possess anything toward persons in need. To quote St. Ambrose: "You are not making a gift of your possessions to the poor person. You are handing over to him what is his. For what has been given in common for the use of all, you have arrogated to yourself. The world is given to all, and not only to the rich" (De Nabuthe, c. 12, n. 53; PL 14, 747). That is, *private property does not constitute for anyone* an absolute and unconditioned right. No one is justified in keeping for his exclusive use what he does not need, when others lack necessities. In a word, "according to the traditional doctrine as found in the Fathers of the Church and the great theologians, the right to property must never be exercised to the detriment of the common good." If there should arise a conflict "between acquired private rights and primary community exigencies," it is the responsibility of public authorities "to look for a solution, with the active participation of individuals and social groups" (n. 23).[19]

In all periods of the Christian era, theological statements can be found which represent an extension of the fundamental biblical insight—namely, that the poor are precious in God's sight, not because they are destitute, but because they have not exploited others. Similarly, the rich risk damnation, not because they have possessions, but only if and because they have exploited others and adamantly refuse to share with those in need.

Human societies have a way of encouraging the repetition of functions in some organized way. We tend, therefore, to allow custom to blind us to inequalities and injustices that result from the "way" we have of "doing things." "That's just the way it is" serves as the ready reply to the questions we occasionally raise about destitution, deprivation and related social ills. Well, the "way it is" often reflects a foundation of social relationships known as a "power structure." If power, the ability to cause or prevent change, is exercised in an organized, repetitive way to create or retain injustice, a sinful social structure is at work. Social sin, as well as personal, can also result from omission. Hence, we have to examine our consciousness not only of what we have done to cause injustice, but also of what we are *not* doing to remove or prevent it. We should, moreover, become familiar with the structures themselves before hoping to do anything about the problems related to them. For instance, there is a criminal justice system in the United States which must be understood before it can be altered to deal more justly with the poor. There are systems or structures of international trade; there is an international monetary system. These must be understood before they can be changed or replaced so that world poverty might be reduced. It is especially important to understand any structure that one might be inclined to destroy.

Wage structures, collective bargaining, welfare systems, political structures, educational systems, trusteeships, highway systems, interest rates, tax rates, retirement benefits—all these and countless other elements in our society are structural components of societal life. They can impede or enhance freedom, equality, order and justice for the people. Behind each element and every structural arrangement of societal elements stands a law. The relationship between law and power is second only to the relationship of wealth to law for strategic importance in translating a Christian theology of poverty into an actual economic empowerment of the poor.

Power and Structure

If a man did not have a bone structure, he would be a puddle of flesh spread unevenly on the ground. If there were no social structures, societal life would be impossible. A social structure is a functional arrangement of human persons for human purposes. It helps people get things done—together. If it gets things done for some unjustly at the expense of others, it is oppressive of those others. The fact that it gets things done at all is indicative, however, of the inextricable link between structure and power. Hence the need for further theological reflection.

In his *Theological Investigations*, Karl Rahner sketches a "Theology of Power."[20] He views power as something quite proper to a human being, enabling a person to act freely, without the previous consent of another. But it is also an ability to interfere with that other. Power comes from God and reflects God, Rahner asserts, but he also notes that power, understood as force, stems from sin. He organizes his reflections on power around three theses. First, power, understood as physical force, is the result of sin and serves as a temptation to sin, a manifestation of sin; it is not necessarily sin itself. Second, power, including physical force, is a gift of God and a reflection of God in the world. Third, the exercise of power is a process either "of salvation or perdition."[21]

Rahner's theses on power generate a theological tension with creative possibilities. A consideration of power as both leading to sin and embodying salvation opens the way for a discussion of oppressive social structures as the embodiment of social sin.

Power can become sin. "And it can demonstrate better than anything else what is the true nature of sin: the desire to be like God, the 'no' to service, the installation of self-will and the finite as the absolute, power for power's sake, which is a sin."[22]

What I have suggested earlier can be made more explicit now. I understand social structures to be institutionalized sets of interdependent relationships which influence social behavior and regulate the life chances available to persons at given times and places. The words "system" and "structure" are often used interchangeably. I tend, however, to favor the use of system as the more comprehensive and general term. Within a given system, a variety of structures (institutionalized arrangements that affect behavior) are found. We have a criminal justice system within which the structure of prison life and the structure of appeals courts are found. We have a capitalistic economic system within which a wage structure operates. In both cases, however, we often speak of the prison system and the wage system. The Christian transformation of institutional arrangements can be viewed as the reform of a social structure or the reform of a social system. Similarly, one can speak of an oppressive structure or an oppressive system. My preference for structure over system is both methodological and ideological. I think analysis and action are sounder if aimed at critical parts (structures) rather than the whole (system). Moreover, in the American context, I do not concede that the entire system (economic or social) is evil. I do believe structural reform within the system is needed in order to facilitate the economic empowerment of the poor.

What is structural sin? In an article on the "Theology of Liberation" in *Chicago Studies*,[23] Canadian theologian Patrick Kerans bases his view of structural sin on an understanding of the imagination which is drawn from William Lynch's *Christ and Prometheus*. "As I use the word," says Lynch, "the imagination is not an aesthetic faculty. . . . It is all the resources of man, all his faculties, his whole history, his whole life, and his whole heritage, all brought to bear upon the concrete world inside and outside himself, to form images of the world, and thus to find it, cope with it, shape it, even make it."[24] Continuing, Lynch asserts: "Our images are not the innocent, purely objective things they seem to be. The most casual image contains the whole of man. Images are not snapshots of reality. Everything in us pours into the simplest image. They are ourselves."[25]

Where do the images that shape and control our institutional arrangements come from? From the Gospel? the world? our sinful side? Could it be that poverty is a social expression of our sinfulness? Social arrangements that perpetuate the enrichment of some at the unjust expense of others reflect the greed of those who benefit from them and the sloth of those who do nothing to change them. They are social structures because they are institutionalized sets of interdependent human relationships. They are sinful social structures because they not only embody our greed but survive as a result of our hard-heartedness and sloth. They reduce the "life chances" of the oppressed and they imperil the eternal "life chances" of the oppressors. Patrick Kerans has put it this way:

For if society is a human construction, it makes sense to speak of structural social sin which is quite a different reality than a conspiracy of evil men. I have pointed to the imaginative framework which shapes each person's perception of reality, which when it takes away peace or a sense of self-worth, or when it impels to sin or—worse—rationalizes sin, I would call structural sin.[26]

Viewed in the context of sin and redemption, the poverty problem, with all its derivative damage to human dignity and freedom, should frighten us who deny our complicity while admitting our concern. Perhaps that fright will progress to fear, the kind of fear that has been called "the mother of morality," and then, perhaps, some changes will occur. But change, we know, implies power. And power, I would argue, resides in the middle class. The middle class must come to recognize the power it has and then become aware of what Rahner sees as a salvation-perdition tension confronting all parties to the exercise of power.

Harold D. Lasswell identified an interpersonal characteristic of power that should be noted here:

The accent is on power and the powerful. But it would be a mistake to imagine that in consequence we are wholly taken up with the few rather than the many. Speaking of power and the powerful is an ellipsis, leaving out perhaps what is the longest arc of the circle constituting a power relationship. Power is an interpersonal situation; those who hold power are empowered. They depend upon and continue only so long as there is a continuing stream of empowering responses. Even a casual inspection of human relations will convince any competent observer that power is not a brick that can be lugged from place to place, but a process that vanishes when the supporting responses cease.[27]

Poverty will vanish when the supporting responses cease—support, that is, for the inequitable distribution of privileges, possessions, and power.

In the American political system, the middle class stands in an empowering relationship to the powerful. Governments tend to be stable here because of the middle class. When this stability amounts to insensitivity to the needs of the poor, governmental solutions will not be forthcoming. If this nation's extremes were to get larger than its middle, social repression or social revolution could result, neither offering any better hope than we now have for a just distribution of income, wealth, and economic power in our country. The middle-class mechanisms now in place could do the job if the mechanisms were activated. A moral force is needed to get the process going.

Also standing in an empowering relationship to the

wealthy in this nation are the poor themselves. Hence the economic empowerment of the poor must involve what Paulo Freire has called the "conscientization" of the poor themselves. Their consciousness must be raised to an awareness that they do in fact empower the rich, at least to some extent. When their "supporting responses" cease (as in historical examples of industrial strikes), the power will begin to shift their way. Not enough, perhaps, to really change things. Without similar consciousness-raising involving the middle class, and parallel adjustment of its "supporting responses," there will be no significant improvement for the poor.

It will be a challenge for the Church to work with the middle class, talking tax reform and redistribution where the middle class will not be the direct beneficiary. It will be even more of a challenge for the Church to confront the rich and powerful with the Gospel message. Pope Paul understands the problem well. As Cardinal Montini in May 1959, he told the Catholic exhibitors at the Milan Fair: "It is far easier to speak of the solutions of social questions to the working classes than it is to you (businessmen); to them the solution promises improvements, but from you it demands sacrifices."

And it will be a challenge for the Church to guide and guard the poor as they gain power and prosperity; they are not immune to avarice, greed, and the abuse of power.

In attempting to meet these challenges, the Church will, I suspect, hear itself enunciating in clearer terms the moral principle that where basic life chances are concerned, one simply must not take an unreasonable gain at the expense of another. This moral principle will be reinforced by the scriptural insight that gaining at the expense of another is, in fact, a form of infidelity to the covenant God has made with us. The Christian's response in faith to God will involve a free participation in the economic empowerment of the poor. This is a possibility. Another possibility, taking explicit account of the international scope of the question, is contained in a warning from Frantz Fanon: "The question which is looming on the horizon is the need for a redistribution of wealth. Humanity must reply to this question, or be shaken to pieces by it."

NOTES

1. August 5, 1972, p. 54.
2. *Ibid.*
3. The *Jerome Biblical Commentary* states: "This stanza sings with the ecstatic joy of Dt-Is; the poet is continually crying out 'rejoice!' to messianic Jerusalem. All children of God nurse at the breast of Jerusalem—an image that beautifully portrays universal peace, contentment, and love. Imperceptibly, the image changes and God takes the place of Jerusalem —fondling, comforting and nursing his children" (Englewood Cliffs, N.J.: Prentice-Hall, Inc., 1968, Sec. 22, No. 69, p. 385).
4. See Robert Bierstedt, "An Analysis of Social Power," *American Sociological Review*, 15 (1950), pp. 730-738.
5. I am thinking here of the American middle class. America will do little to assist the poor abroad if middle-class Americans remain uninterested in Third World needs. Power (and, therefore, the ability to block progress for the poor) also resides in the middle class of some foreign nations. There are indications that the fall of the Allende government in Chile in the fall of 1973 was a middle-class revolt.
6. Delivered at the Poverty Conference, Maryland Province, Society of Jesus, Wernersville, Pennsylvania, August 28, 1972.

7. *Op. cit.*, p. 2. "One must consider the great transformation in Israelite society that is implied in the reigns of Solomon and David: in a few generations there was a transition from tribal federation to 'empire' status; the agricultural and pastoral life yielded to urban life with a corresponding growth of social inequalities. In this period Albright estimates a possible Israelite population of 800,000" (Addison G. Wright, S.S., Roland E. Murphy, O. Carm., and Joseph A. Fitzmyer, S.J., "A History of Israel," *Jerome Biblical Commentary, op. cit.*, p. 681). See also Pierre Biard, "Biblical Teaching on Poverty," *Cross Currents*, Fall 1964, pp. 437-438: "The Israel of the poor man is a communitarian Israel."

8. Walsh, *op. cit.*, p. 1.

9. *Ibid.*, pp. 4-5.

10. *Ibid.*

11. This is Joseph Fitzmyer's translation of Phil. 2:6-7. See the *Jerome Biblical Commentary, op. cit.*, Sec. 50, No. 18, p. 250.

12. *Op. cit.*, p. 7. "What I have been talking about negatively as 'letting go,' renunciation of power, giving up any claim to be something on one's own, is of course one side of the coin. The other side is the fact that God is revealed in Christ as love. Love and grasping, 'power-tripping,' *getting*, are mutually exclusive. And the fruits of love—forgiveness, service, trust—are possible only through the kind of self-emptying death we symbolize in the cross. And the paradox . . . is that the powerlessness embodied in Jesus is powerful. It is able to rebuke the evil spirit, bring new life to people dead to love, still the wind and sea; it is, in the terms of the Song of Songs 8:6, 'stronger than death' " (*Ibid.*).

13. See George H. Dunne, S.J., "The Missionary in China—Past, Present, Future," A Paper Delivered at the International Symposium on Ignatian Spirituality and Reform, University of San Francisco, July 16, 1973; distributed by Lutheran World Federation, 150 route de Ferney, 1211 Geneva 20, Switzerland (mimeographed), p. 24.

14. *Liberation, Development and Salvation* (Maryknoll, N.Y.: Orbis Books, 1972), p. 95.

15. *Ibid.*, p. 99.

16. *Ibid.*, p. 95.

17. *Ibid.*, p. 96.

18. *Ibid.*, pp. 97-98.

19. The portions of the Pope's text which are in quotation marks are taken from his Letter to the 51st Session of the French Social Weeks (Lyons, 1964); see *L'Osservatore Romano*, July 10, 1964.

20. Vol. IV (Baltimore: Helicon Press, 1966), pp. 391-409.

21. *Ibid.*, p. 395.

22. *Ibid., p. 406.*

23. Vol. XI, No. 2 (Summer 1972), pp. 183-195.

24. *Ibid.,* p. 187.

25. *Ibid.*

26. *Ibid.*, p. 194.

27. *Power and Personality* (New York: Viking Press, 1962), p. 10 (originally published by Norton, 1948).

3. The Environment and Social Justice

Toward a Theology of Stewardship

The conjunction of environment and social justice implies a principle that is both ethical and ecological. I take it as a first law of environmental science that everything is connected with everything else. Ecology is concerned with the interrelationship of organisms and their environment. Hence an ecological consciousness would be an awareness of the interrelationship of all living things.

The same notion of interrelatedness applies in theology and ethics. A theology of human solidarity helps to explain not only our inheritance of original sin, but also our liberation from sin through the sacrifice of the God-man who died for all. From this fact, St. John concludes that those who are thus redeemed must be especially concerned about one another: "He laid down his life for us; and we likewise ought to lay down our life for the brethren" (1 Jn. 3:16). Consequently, a theology of our human solidarity or interrelatedness includes the notion of moral obligation toward all others with whom we are, by virtue of a common human nature and a universal redemptive act, locked, so to speak, hand-in-hand around the world.

This present reflection, however, focuses not on my direct interaction with other human beings through the mechanisms of right and obligation in a moral universe, but rather on my indirect relationship to them *through the environment*. This is not to say that I have no theological regard for the environment in its own right, that I consider the land only in reference to man. Genesis does, it should be noted, refer to all that God created as being indeed "very good" (Gen. 1:31). I wouldn't want to alter that. But I do regard land *for man* as the primary perspective theologically and even ecologically—not forgetting, however, that while man is distinguishable from the rest of creation he is not separable from it.

Let me mention in passing that there is a present danger, from a theological perspective, associated with those manifestations of contemporary ecological consciousness which tend to substitute reverence *for* nature for a reverence through nature. The long and solid contemplative tradition of "finding God in all things" or letting nature "mirror the creator" is alive and well and useful today, but useful, theologically speaking, insofar as it brings man in contact with God, not simply with nature.

Thorkild Jacobsen suggests that in the opening lines of Psalm 19, "nature appears bereaved of divinity before an absolute God."[1] To the psalmist, the heavens only witness to God's greatness; they do not contain him. "The heavens declare the glory of God, the vault of heaven proclaims his handiwork" (Ps. 19:1). To the ancient Mesopotamians, says Jacobsen, the heavens are the "very majesty of godhead, the highest ruler, Anu."[2]

The God of the psalmists and prophets transcended nature, indicating, and this is Jacobsen's point, that the Hebrews and Greeks broke with the mode of speculation that had prevailed up to their time. My point is that the contemporary back-to-nature impulse of ecological consciousness is in some instances a return to the ancient view that the divine was wholly immanent in nature. This could be a regression to paganism, something quite distinct from a secular declaration that the heavens are empty and God is absent, if not dead. Such declarations prepare the way for the establishment of ecology as a religion in its own right. We've been through that already in America with patriotism-as-religion; not again now with ecology!

In any case, my present concern is man's indirect moral relationship to other men through the environment. This implies a direct relationship of man to the environment which I shall describe in the context of a theology of stewardship.

The Bible leaves little doubt that the world is made for man and man is made for God. Man's mission in the world is to complete creation: "Be fruitful and multiply, and fill the earth and subdue it; and have dominion over the fish of the sea and over the birds of the air and over every living thing that moves upon the earth" (Gen. 1:28). This verse, the centerpiece in Lynn White's famous argument that Christianity and the rejection of pagan animism make it possible for Western man "to exploit nature in a mood of indifference to the feelings of natural objects,"[3] is a conclusion to the proposition stated in Genesis 1:26: "Then God said, 'Let us make man in our image, after our likeness.' " Because he is created in God's image, man's nature, flowing from the nature of God, is to exercise dominion over creation, and in developing creation to complete himself in his cycle out and back from God through the world.[4] As he cultivates creation and builds this world, man is not "working off" the penalty of the fall; he is exercising fidelity to the true meaning of man who is created in the image of a creator God.

Genesis 1:28—God's command to man to "subdue" the earth and "have dominion" over fish and birds and all the rest—must be read in conjunction with Genesis 2:15: "Yahweh God took the man and settled him in the Garden of Eden to cultivate and take care of it." "Take care" is more than a colloquial conclusion to countless passing conversations; it is an ancient mandate to man the cultivator-builder.

Man is not the creator, not the *Dominus*. The dominion he exercises is delegated power. He is a steward, not an owner. He tends to forget this. A corrective for this tendency is found in the Book of Deuteronomy in both the 6th and 8th chapters. To cite one example which makes particularly interesting reading to those fond of thinking of America as a "promised land":

But Yahweh your God is bringing you into a prosperous land, a land of streams and springs, of waters that well up from the deep in valleys and hills, a land of wheat and barley, of vines, of figs, of pomegranates, a land of olives, of oil, of honey, a land where you will eat bread without stint, where you will want nothing, a land where the stones are of iron, where the hills may be quarried for copper. You will eat and have all you want, and you will bless Yahweh your God in the rich land he has given you.

Take care you do not forget Yahweh your God, neglecting his commandments and customs and laws which I lay on you today. When you have eaten and have all you want, when you have built fine houses to live in, when you have seen your flocks and herds increase, your silver and gold abound and all your possessions grow great, do not become proud of heart. Do not then forget Yahweh your God who brought you out of the land of Egypt, out of the house of slavery, who guided you through this vast and dreadful wilderness. . . . Beware of saying in your heart, "My own strength and the might of my own hand won this power for me." Remember Yahweh your God: it was he who gave you this strength and won you this power, thus keeping the covenant then, as today, that he swore to your fathers. Be sure that if you forget Yahweh your God, you will most certainly perish (Dt. 8:7-19).

We are stewards of the land, water and air given to us by God. They are ours to use, but how can the argument be made that they are intended by God to be available to meet the needs of all? This argument must be made if I am to link man to man in a relationship of social justice through the environment. This cannot be done satisfactorily without moving the argument forward through the New Testament and at least on to the patristic period. But before attempting that, I want to borrow from Jacobsen's description of the concept of stewardship in the Mesopotamian city-state, a private organization whose primary purpose was economic, distinguishing it from the national state with its primarily political purpose.[5] Our modern concept of a sovereign, independent state is not helpful here. The ancient Mesopotamian world-view saw the gods owning the land, and man, since no human organization can be sovereign and independent, serving the gods. "Therefore, no human institution can have its primary aim in the welfare of its own human members; it must seek primarily the welfare of the gods."[6] To move to the conclusion that ancient and Old Testament thought saw man obliged to use the land in service to his fellow man, it would be convenient if ancient pagan literature or the Old Testament contained statements resembling the remark of Walter Rauschenbusch that "when we hold property in trust for God, we hold it for humanity, of which we are a part." Unfortunately, the "welfare of the gods" in the Mesopotamian world-view was not always identical with the good of mankind.

Nonetheless, the city was central to the Mesopotamian city-state, and the temple of the city god was central to the city and usually owned most of the land in the state. It is estimated that around the middle of the third millennium B.C., most of the lands of a Mesopotamian city-state were temple lands.[7] They were cultivated by serfs and sharecroppers.

These human toilers, whether sharecroppers, serfs, or temple servants, shepherds, brewers, or cooks, were organized in groups under human overseers in a hierarchy which culminated in the highest human servant of the god, the *ensi*, manager of the god's estate and manager of his city-state.

We call the *ensi* "manager" of the god's estate; and his position vis-à-vis the god was actually closely parallel to that of an estate manager, a steward vis-à-vis the owner. A steward appointed to manage an estate is expected, first of all, to uphold and carry on the established order of that estate; secondly, he is to execute such specific commands as the owner may see fit to give with respect to changes, innovations, or ways to deal with unexpected situations. Quite similarly, the *ensi* was expected to uphold the established order of the god's temple and city in general, but he was expected to consult the god and carry out any specific orders which the god might wish to give.[8]

Two observations at this juncture. (1) Admitting that my search has been in no way exhaustive, I simply assert that a doctrine of the use of land for the good of humanity is unavailable in the pagan literature and at least not clear in the Old Testament. (2) The ancient alertness on the part of the steward "to consult the god and carry out any specific orders which the god might wish to give" might be profitably resurrected today in a renewed sensitivity to Christian discernment of spirits and the quest to discover revelations of God's will in contemporary events. God might just be interested in clarifying for us the choices that must be made if we are to avoid eco-catastrophe.

Moving now to a New Testament perspective of our question, reference can be made to the parable of the talents and the story of the unjust steward to argue that Jesus assumes that we hold our resources in trust and that they are not ours to use absolutely. But to what extent may we argue, on scriptural evidence, that we hold these resources in trust for others?

According to St. Luke, "A man in the crowd said to him, 'Master, tell my brother to give me a share of our inheritance.' 'My friend,' he replied, 'who appointed me your judge, or the arbitrator of your claims?' Then he said to them, 'Watch and be on your guard against avarice of any kind, for a man's life is not made secure by what he owns, even when he has more than he needs' " (Lk. 12:13-15). Following this reply is the parable about the man whose harvest was good and who planned to build bigger barns to store his goods and then "take things easy, eat and drink and have a good time," unaware that "this very night the demand will be made for your soul" (Lk. 12:20). Neither in the reply nor in the parable does Jesus suggest a doctrine of stewardship of wealth for the good of others. Discipleship is much more a matter of giving up possessions than using them for others. As a matter of fact, the "crafty" or "unjust" steward of the parable that opens Luke's 16th chapter uses his stewardship *dishonestly* in easing the burdens of others!

The parable of the talents (Mt. 25:14-30) or the pounds (Lk. 19:11-28) makes it clear that the owner of the land puts severe demands on those to whom he entrusts his goods. (God, the owner, expects much of us, his servants, serfs, sharecroppers, or stewards.) And with the practice of fidelity comes even greater responsibility, according to the Gospel message.

Such scriptural evidence supports the conjecture if not the precise conclusion that man is expected to interact with his environment responsibly, in fidelity to the trust bestored on him by God. Moreover, man's responsibility today is, negatively speaking, to avert the loss of land, air and water and other natural resources through irresponsible use that would not simply bury these "talents" but diminish or destroy them. But there is no clear and specific scriptural mandate to use the land for others. This comes, however, with the earliest pronouncements of the teaching Church.

In the *Didache*, an instruction written by an unknown author very early in the Christian era to summarize the sayings of Jesus as taught by the apostles in their missionary journeys, the following doctrine is communicated:

Give to anyone that asks you, and demand no return; the Father wants his own bounties to be shared with all. Happy the giver who complies with the commandment, for he goes unpunished. Trouble is in store for the receiver: if someone who is in need receives, he will go unpunished; but he who is not in need will have to stand trial as to why and for what purpose he received. . . . Let your alms sweat in your hands until you find out to whom to give (1:5-6).

And later:

Do not be one that opens his hands to receive, but shuts them when it comes to giving. If you have means at your disposal, pay a ransom for your sins. Do not hesitate to give, and do not give in a grumbling mood. You will find out who is the good Rewarder. Do not turn away from the needy; rather share everything with your brother, and do not say: "It is private property." If you are sharers in what is imperishable, how much more so in the things that perish (4:5-8).

The reference here to private property reflects the ideal of early Christian communitarian living described in the Acts of the Apostles (Acts 2:44-45). Here in Acts, as in many other biblical texts, the needy are singled out for attention and assistance. To care for or share with the needy is a common demand made upon the believer.

Negatively, Old and New Testament alike warn against avarice of any kind. Both notions—avarice and the needy—provide the early Church Fathers with doctrinal material that they apply to the problem of poverty. Both notions appear in magisterial pronouncements, most recently and notably in *Gaudium et Spes* and *Populorum Progressio*.

I would like to suggest that ecological accents might appropriately be placed today on these themes of avoidance of avarice and assistance to the needy. Destruction of the environment is avaricious behavior in the sense that mindless consumption and exploitation of resources which were intended by God to be available in some way to all is sinfully self-centered, greedy, shortsighted activity. It denies others access to these resources now, and even destroys these resources in the absence of adequate recycling processes, thus denying future generations even the chance of access.

And who could be more needy than a future (possibly not-too-distant future) inhabitant of our city or our planet whose land has been despoiled and not replenished, whose water and air are polluted beyond repair?

The early Church Fathers came down hard on those who selfishly refused to share their goods with the needy.[9] "Feed the man dying of hunger, because if you have not fed him, you have killed him" is patristic doctrine that the Fathers of the Second Vatican Council saw fit to repeat in their *Pastoral Constitution on the Church in the Modern World.*[10] Perhaps some modern bishops will take to their pulpits soon and keep this kind of oratory alive with an exhortation to "help the man gasping for pure air, or searching for potable water, for if you have not helped him you have killed him." And when will such exhortations be too late, simply because environmental destruction has reached a point of irreversibility?[11] St. John Chrysostom, the greatest orator and perhaps the strongest social critic among the early Greek Fathers, probably never dreamed of an ecological crisis. Yet his words strike a keynote for the kind of moral exhortation needed today: "Do not say 'I am using what belongs to me.' You are using what belongs to others. All the wealth of the world belongs to you and to others in common, as do sun, air, earth, and all the rest."[12]

What are the practical issues now? What now must be done?

With the focus fixed on the American environment, the general issue was well stated in a recent speech by Senator Howard Baker, famous for his position on the Watergate Committee but also the ranking Republican member of the Senate Committee on Public Works, at the annual convention of the American Paper Institute in New York City:

It will no doubt be recorded that the United States in the twentieth century achieved a degree of technical expertise and industrial capacity that improved the material well-being of our citizens.

It must not also be said that in doing so we squandered our natural resources, and in raising our standard of living we contributed to lowering our quality of life.

Only in this decade has environmental quality truly become a cause of national concern. Through the nearly two hundred years of our history, we have depended primarily on the natural recycling system of our air and water to absorb the large quantities of the pollutants as by-products of our industrial development.

Our growing population and burgeoning industry economy have in this century put strains on our natural purification system. The bill for years of neglect is now coming due, itemized in the headlines chronicling eco-catastrophes.[13]

Behind our problems with the domestic environment are the issues of economic growth, population growth and population density. Radical (as distinguished from liberal or conservative) economic analysis would insist that (1) environmental destruction is an inevitable consequence of the high priority attached to economic growth in capitalistic societies, and that (2) technological advance has a way of bringing with it unforeseen deleterious ecological effects. Since capitalism will never give up the goal of growth or accept a moratorium on technological innovation, "the system," according to the radical critique, will continue to produce pollution.[14]

Economists at the Brookings Institution in Washington, D.C., blending elements of a conservative and a liberal economic analysis, believe that "stopping growth is an unnecessary and excessively costly means of controlling pollution."[15] They see nothing in the nature of air or water pollution that would call for a halt to economic growth as a necessary remedy. Continued growth in the Gross National Product would, at present annual rates of economic growth, generate by 1980 at least five times more additional income than the amount needed to meet stringent clean-up standards for our air and water. "In other words, by devoting only a fraction of the increase in the GNP over the next eight years to environmental control purposes, the nation could achieve stringent control standards and still have very substantial gains in living standards, as conventionally defined."[16] The problem, of course, is that of the political will to apply significant percentages of that increased income to the battle against pollution. It might also be remarked that attention should be paid to the composition of growth before prescribing a blanket ban. A growth that expands non-polluting services or produces pollution-reducing equipment is quite different from production that is destructive of the environment. Even a critic like scientist George M. Woodwell who chides the growth advocates for their assumption that "the environment has an assimilation capacity for all human insults"[17] says:

The inevitable restriction of growth in energy-dense activities does not restrict growth in all segments of society. On the contrary, the problems present an intellectual challenge unprecedented in history. We have now a great new freedom to examine in detail the enduring question of what man's most rewarding circumstance might be. On these topics growth has barely begun.[18]

In a study paper prepared for the Executive Council of the United Church of Christ to help in the education of UCC membership to the need for a reordering of national priorities, Roger Strait and Paul T. Stames state that with the arrival of the environmental crisis, "the American Dream has lost the freedom of irresponsibility."[19] Unless we realize fast the dream of a just and equitable society, "the problems of pollution and lack of growth will preclude its possibility."[20] Our prospects for eliminating poverty and disease depend on further economic growth. The authors agree that our present margin of growth should be applied to the solution of the poverty problem. Moreover, that margin of growth can be extended "to the degree that we funnel funds into a rigorous recycling and into basic research for new and cleaner sources of energy."[21]

The environmental issue, as so many other issues in social ethics, comes into sharp relief when positioned against the pocketbook question: Who will pay the bill? Most of the sources of air and water pollution are found in private industry. It may be presumed, therefore, that most of the costs of the clean-up and future prevention will be added to the prices consumers pay for the products of the polluting industries. These costs will not be added to the federal budget. While the federal government will face rising costs of its own due to increased regulatory activities, research, technical assistance and subsidies to private industry, it will contribute to a rise in industrial costs by imposing emission or effluent taxes, penalty fees, license fees, and recycling responsibilities ("If you made it, you've got to take it back in its waste stage"), and by reforming the present tax system which now favors the industrial use of virgin materials instead of recycled materials; such reform would raise costs to those who shun the use of recycled material.[22]

In attempting to control pollution, government has a basic choice between the regulatory route or the application of economic incentives to the problem. The Brookings study cited earlier favors the latter approach. Taxes or "effluent charges" on each unit of pollution passing from industry into the air or water "would provide business firms with an incentive to reduce pollution in order to lower their tax burden."[23] The firm will remove the pollution up to the point where the cost of doing so exceeds the amount of the tax, the effluent charge. A higher tax would encourage a purer effluent. "The kinds of products whose manufacture generated a lot of pollution would become more expensive and would carry higher prices than those that generated less, and consumers would be induced to buy more of the latter."[24]

As long as there is a unit of pollution in the product, a corresponding effluent charge will be levied against the producer—hence the economic incentive to have a pollution-free product. But either the cost of removing pollution, or the penalty tax (the effluent charge) associated with the polluting product, will be passed along to the consumer. Will this "pollution tax" be acceptable to the American taxpayer who already considers his taxes to be too high? The 1973 shock of a national fuel shortage forced Americans to face some unpleasant economic realities. As a people, we have a tendency to forget that we can't have everything we want. And the things we like, and grow accustomed to, cannot be presumed to be available in an endless supply. As the fuel crisis forces a recognition that our life-style cannot be maintained without higher costs to ourselves, perhaps we will come to see that simplifying our life-style could reduce the costs of our way of life to others. For, as we have been consuming more and more of the world's non-renewable resources, less has been available to serve the needs of others. Our accelerating consumption has, moreover, produced our pollution. The energy crisis may be a blessing in disguise. It could force us into a simpler consumption pattern that will put us, despite our protests, back on the road to survival.

A contemporary theology of stewardship would support higher prices ("taxes") for pollution reduction, insisting all the while on productive efficiency and that some of the added costs should be offset by profit reductions, and not solely by higher prices to the consumer. A theology of stewardship would also support reduced consumption of scarce resources. In any case, a contemporary theology of stewardship might attempt to apply an unpopular passage in Pope Paul VI's *Populorum Progressio* to the present situation. Extending (without bending the papal thought) the notion of "most destitute" to a near-future generation in need of unpolluted earth, air and water, "development" to man's hoped-for conquest of pollution in order to survive, and "the rich" to those who now command, control or consume disproportionately large shares of the world's resources, I suggest that the Pope's words have special moral significance in the environmental crisis:

Let each one examine his conscience, a conscience that conveys a new message in our times. Is he prepared to support out of his own pocket works and undertakings organized in favor of the most destitute? Is he ready to pay higher taxes so that the public authorities can intensify their efforts in favor of development?[25]

Pope Paul continues:

We must repeat once more that the superfluous wealth of rich countries should be placed at the service of poor countries. The rule which up to now held good for the benefit of those nearest to us must today be applied to all the needy of the world. Besides the rich will be the first to benefit as a result. Otherwise their continued greed will certainly call down upon them the judgment of God and the wrath of the poor, with consequences no one can foretell.[26]

We are back again to the notions of greed and need. On his guard against avarice and mindful of the needs of others, the American consumer should be prepared to support out of his own pocket the protection and repair of the environment. He should be ready to shift his preferences toward those products that issue from a pollution-free process. His readiness in this regard can be a form of reverence for creation, for the creator and for the neighbor in need, as well as for the generation yet unborn.[27] And all of this would be an exercise of stewardship.

My initial observation that ecological interrelatedness has an ethical parallel—one's moral relationship to others through the environment—is repeated now at the conclusion of this reflection. My life span need not overlap with that of any of these "others" for some ethical interrelationship to exist. Present ecological indicators suggest that some future generation may well be the neediest of all generations, deprived of air, water, mineral resources, and cultivable land. Present human activity could contribute to the destruction of the environment that would otherwise have provided life support for that future generation. Associated with such present human activity, therefore, is a moral responsibility. A related responsibility exists now with respect to population control. It is, as Daniel Callahan suggests, "at least conceivably possible that the present generation could so heavily populate the earth that it would be impossible for that earth to sustain the large numbers of people which would result from a continuation of high population growth rates."[28] It was a sense of present moral urgency that prompted the Federation of Asian Bishops Conference (a Roman Catholic assembly) to declare: "We regard the population problem as a very great and urgent one, demanding immediate and effective solutions. . . . We also believe that the Church in Asia must contribute to and support the enlightened efforts of governments in programs of population control and of socio-economic development."[29]

Economic growth, population growth and population density stand, as I have already said, behind our environmental problems. Social justice calls now for responsible human activity that is both reparative and preventative. Radical human responses are called for. Curiously, the most radical device available to us may be the age-old notion of stewardship—the idea that no man owns anything absolutely, that everything is held in trust. Admittedly, the application of the stewardship concept to the problems of population growth and density is, at best, ambiguous. But it fits the problem of economic growth. And the exercise of genuine stewardship by man with respect to all his material assets may not only help the poor and protect the environment, but sensitize the "steward" to the inhumane consequences of greater population density and the destructive potential of a rate of increase that doubles the world population every thirty-five years.

The relationship may be ambiguous, but stewardship can apply to population issues as well as to our care for earth, air, water and all non-renewable resources. The link is suggested in lines from an Aztec prayer: ". . . and even the sounds of the waterfall die out in the dry season; so we, too, because only for a short time have you loaned us to each other."

NOTES

1. *Before Philosophy: The Intellectual Adventure of Ancient Man* (Pelican, 1949), p. 262.

2. *Ibid.*, p. 237.

3. "The Historical Roots of Our Ecologic Crisis," *Science*, Vol. 155, No. 3767 (March 10, 1973), p. 1205.

4. For a development of this point, see Rene Laurentin, *Liberation, Development and Salvation* (Maryknoll, N.Y.: Orbis, 1972), pp. 71-73.

5. *Op. cit.*, pp. 200-207.

6. *Ibid.*, p. 200.

7. *Ibid.*, p. 201.

8. *Ibid.*, p. 203.

9. See, for example, St. Basil's Homily on Avarice in Migne, *Patrologiae Cursus Completus*, (Paris, 1885), p. 275.

10. *Gaudium et Spes*, n. 69.

11. For a sobering indication that such a point of irreversibility is approaching, see George M. Woodwell, "Ecological Effects of Growth," testimony before the Senate Subcommittee on Air and Water Pollution, April 2, 1973; reprinted in the *Congressional Record*, 93rd Congress, 1st Session, Vol. 119, No. 51 (April 3, 1973), pp. S6488-6491.

Dr. Woodwell, of the Brookhaven National Laboratory, discusses "the dependence of man on the earth's living resources. I believe that the data I shall summarize indicates that this dependence is far greater than the world's intellectual, political or economic leaders have commonly acknowledged, that irreversible changes are occurring at the moment that have great importance for all, and that, while significant steps have been taken recently in our air and water pollution bills, much more powerful steps are needed to prevent major, irreversible changes in the capacity of the earth for the support of man" (p. S6488).

12. *On First Corinthians*, Homily 10, ch. 3.

13. *Congressional Record*, 93rd Congress, 1st Session, Vol. 119, No. 45 (March 22, 1973), p. S5502.

14. See David Gorden, ed., *Problems in Political Economy* (Lexington, Mass.: D. C. Heath, 1971) pp. 451-455.

15. See Charles L. Schultze *et al., Setting National Priorities: The 1973 Budget* (Washington: Brookings, 1972), p. 375.

16. *Ibid.*, p. 375.

17. *Op. cit.* (see note 11 above), p. S6490.

18. *Ibid.*, p. S6491.

19. *Issues, Costs and Benefits of New Priorities* (Philadelphia: United Church Board for Homeland Ministries, 1972), p. 18.

20. *Ibid.*

21. *Ibid.*, p. 19.

22. "The Environmental Protection Agency recently published an important study on resource recovery. Using figures compiled by the Midwest Research Institute, EPA came to the conclusion that for the paper industry the manufacturing of 1,000 tons of pulp from repulped paper waste would mean 61 percent less water pollution, 70 percent less air pollution, and a 70 percent reduction in energy consumption, compared with the manufacturing of a similar 1,000 tons of unbleached kraft pulp. A similar range of savings are available in other industries. To make 1,000 tons of steel, the steel industry could reduce its energy use by 75 percent, its air pollution by 86 percent, and its water pollution by 76 percent, if it used exclusively scrap steel rather than virgin ores. We in the Congress have some tough decisions ahead. We must en-

courage recycling without disastrous impact on our basic industries" (Senator Howard Baker, *op. cit.*, p. S5503).

23. Charles L. Schultze *et al., op. cit.*, p. 369.

24. *Ibid.*, p. 372.

25. Pope Paul VI, *On the Development of Peoples* (Washington, D.C.: U.S. Catholic Conference, 1967), n. 47, p. 35.

26. *Ibid.*, n. 49, p. 36.

27. For further reflection on this last point, see Daniel Callahan, "What Obligations Do We Have to Future Generations?" *American Ecclesiastical Review*, Vol. CLXIV, No. 4 (April 1971), pp. 265-280.

28. *Ibid.*, p. 273.

29. Quoted in Jaime Bulatao, S.J., "Population, Culture and Christianity," a paper presented at the meeting of The Jesuit Missions Board of Directors, New Orleans, La., October 17-18, 1973; reprinted in *Jesuit Missions Newsletter*, No. 29 (November 1973), p. 6.

4.   The Poor: Always With Us?

"All my life I've had only one idea—if a guy did anything for anybody else, he was a sucker" (Humphrey Bogart in "The Big Shot").

"Yet he was pierced through for our faults, crushed for our sins. On him lies a punishment that brings us peace, and through his wounds, we are healed" (Is. 53:5).

"You have the poor with you always, and you can be kind to them whenever you wish, but you will not always have me" (Mk. 14:7-8).

On November 11, 1973, the 22nd Sunday after Pentecost and the 32nd Ordinary Sunday of the Year, liturgical assemblies throughout the Catholic world heard Scripture readings from the First Book of Kings (17:10-16), the Letter to the Hebrews (9:24-28), and the Gospel of Mark (12:38-44). As a homilist that Sunday in a parish church in the most affluent section of New Orleans, I first reminded the congregation that other Scripture passages indicate that "true religion" consists in caring for widows and orphans. The readings from 1 Kings and Mark, proclaimed that Sunday, added, I said, a "frighteningly beautiful refinement" to that notion of "true religion." In those readings we find widows—symbolically the neediest in need of help—caring for the needs of others. Their example is beautiful, as any act of generous sharing is beautiful to behold. Their example is frighteningly beautiful because, comparing their giving to our own, we can only conclude that we do not share, do not give enough.

The story from the First Book of Kings deals with generosity and sharing in very graphic terms. Elijah sees a widow gathering sticks and says to her: "Please bring me a small cupful of water to drink." As she went to get it, he called after her: "Please bring along a bit of bread." She turns slowly and, calling upon God to witness the truth of her reply, answers that she has only a handful of flour; she was collecting these sticks to build a fire in order to prepare a last meal for herself and her son. They are so destitute, she says, they will eat this last meal and die. They have reached the end of hope. Elijah reassures her, telling her not to be afraid but to use that bit of flour to bake a cake for *him*. "Then you can prepare something for yourself and your son." *"Then"*—i.e., after she has used the only flour and oil she has; next comes the prediction-fulfillment[1] part of the story. Elijah, the prophet, tells her: "The Lord, the God of Israel says, 'The jar of flour shall not go empty, nor the jug of oil run dry, until the day when the Lord sends rain upon the earth.' " Apparently, the shortage of flour was due to drought, not waste or unwillingness to work. As the saying goes, she was really "up against it."

The story continues with the widow doing as Elijah said. Miraculously, both she and her son were able to eat for a year. "The jar of flour did not go empty, nor the jug of oil run dry, as the Lord had foretold through Elijah" (1 Kgs. 17:16).

Throughout the Elijah cycle of the Book of Kings,

prediction-fulfillment sayings occur. In this case, it is predicted that the widow's generosity will win for her a reward. Her willingness to share the last food she had would gain for her an abundant return.

The generosity-reward theme is repeated, somewhat subtly, in the second reading of the three proclaimed by the Church that Sunday morning. Hebrews 9:24-28 asserts that the generous Christ shared all that he had—his life—so that we might live. He was down, so to speak, to the last few grains of life, and he shared what was left. It returned to him in resurrected glory, and to us in the life of grace. "He has made his appearance once and for all . . . to do away with sin by sacrificing himself" (Heb. 9:27). Not by giving an order that cost him nothing, nor by a token offering—a tax-deductible contribution—but by his sacrifice, by his death, he gave us life. There is a symbolic identity in this set of readings between the widow and Christ—the neediest in need of help, caring for the needs of others.

The third in this generosity-reward set of Scripture readings offered for reflection at that Sunday liturgy comes from the Gospel of Mark—the story of the widow's mite. Here the lesson comes through in crystal-clear fashion. After putting down ostentatious display, after practically ridiculing those who seek places of honor and look for privileges and respect—in a word, after delivering a stinging blow to the kind of hypocrisy that is all too familiar to most of us—Jesus relates a compelling account of true generosity.

The two small coins dropped by that woman into the collection box in the temple treasury represented a tiny fraction of a laborer's daily wage in Jerusalem at this time. This was all she had to live on. Jesus seized upon the opportunity to make a point of enormous significance for all who would follow him: "I tell you solemnly, this poor widow has put *more* in than all who have contributed to the treasury; for they have all put in money they had over, but she from the little she has put in everything she possessed, all she had to live on" (Mk. 13:43-44).

The measure of generosity is not what you give, according to this lesson, but what you give measured against what you have. Quite obviously, from a quantitative point of view, Jesus could not have truthfully said she gave more than all the others. But somehow, in a qualitative, spiritual and truly religious sense, she did.

The story, I suggested in my homily on these texts, leaves us unsettled, uncomfortable and disturbed. By the standards of the scribes mentioned earlier in the same Gospel story ("In his teaching he said, 'Beware of the scribes who like to walk about in long robes, to be greeted obsequiously in the market squares, to take the front seats in the synagogues and the places of honor at banquets; these are the men who swallow the property of widows, while making a show of lengthy prayers' "— Mark 12:38-40), by their standards this widow was an absolute fool. By the norms that guide the practical choices of most contemporary Christians, she was imprudent, unwise and foolish. Our reaction to her may help us locate our deepest values. Perhaps we are closer to the value portrayed by Bogart ("All my life I've had only one idea—if a guy did anything for anybody else, he was a sucker") than the value embodied in and encouraged by the person of Christ ("Go and sell everything you own and give the money to the poor, and you will have treasure in heaven; then come, follow me"— Mark 10:21).

In any case, I ended my homily that morning by

mentioning a few points not covered in this Gospel story. We do not know whether the widow benefited in any material way from her generosity. Her gesture has been noted for all posterity, but not her name. There is no way of knowing now whether she had anything to eat that night. Nor do we have the reassurance of knowing that the temple treasury was managed for the benefit of the poor and needy. All we know is that true religion is caring for those in need, and that Jesus used the story of the widow's mite to tell us that the measure of our generosity, indeed of our Christianity, is not what we give, but what we give measured against what we have. Few of us find comfort in that message.

As the parishioners filed past me and on through the church door at the end of Mass that Sunday, there were far fewer handshakes, smiles and comments on the sermon than is ordinarily the case. One young man, a high school science teacher, remarked, "Arithmetically, that Gospel just doesn't add up." An older gentleman took me aside and said, "I don't want to get involved in a theological discussion. But I wonder if you recall the incident where another woman washed our Lord's feet with expensive perfume, and someone asked about the waste, and how the perfume could have been sold and the money given to the poor. You'll remember that our Lord said: 'The poor you will always have with you.' Are you going to preach about that some Sunday?" He was a bit annoyed but not at all hostile or discourteous. We have had many pleasant exchanges on subsequent Sundays as he arrived for Mass or left afterward. As a matter of fact, only a week or two after our first conversation, he came to me before Mass with a conscience problem. He had an early starting time at his golf course that morning, he explained, and he wondered if he could leave Mass immediately after communion and still meet his Sunday obligation.

One way of describing the task of the Church in America today is to get conscientious Christians concerned about the right things.

To play golf with a clear conscience while domestic poverty persists and foreign poverty abounds is to witness to an insensitivity that is inconsistent with the following of Christ. To measure one's fidelity to Christ by scrupulous adherence to a liturgical time-clock is to miss the point of the Christian religion.

Perhaps there will always be some poor people with us. Exegetically, of course, there is no difficulty in handling that famous text.[2] In Mark 14:7-8, Jesus says to his disciples, "You have the poor with you always, and you can be kind to them whenever you wish, but you will not always have me." This is not an invitation to ignore poverty or an excuse to avoid doing anything about it. It is, rather, a comparison chosen by Christ to emphasize to his disciples the brevity of his remaining days on earth over against the long duration of the problem of poverty in the human community. The whole Gospel message calls upon those who possess an abundance of this world's goods to share them with the poor. Refusal to do so imperils salvation. The disciples of Jesus were "astounded" when Jesus said, "How hard it is for those who have riches to enter the kingdom of God" (Mk. 10:23-24). Their astonishment was a predictable response to this radical departure from the Jewish belief that wealth was a sign of God's favor.

In her autobiography, *Times to Remember*, Rose Fitzgerald Kennedy, mother of the late President, tells how press accounts of her husband's wealth in the days when he was advising and supporting Franklin D.

Roosevelt in his quest for the presidency made it necessary for her to explain to her children that their father was well-to-do. "We were careful to emphasize that money brought responsibility. I used to quote from St. Luke to the children, 'To whom much is given, much is required.' Money is never to be squandered or spent ostentatiously."[3]

Much has been given to America and most Americans. Much is now required. Our concern today should be the steady reduction of poverty. Concretely, this means steady progress toward relative egalitarianism. Exegetical problems aside, serious ethical problems remain twenty centuries after Christ remarked, "You have the poor with you always."

Toward Equality

Probably no one has contributed more to economic education in America in the past quarter century than Professor Paul A. Samuelson of the Massachusetts Institute of Technology. His scholarly work has won for him the Nobel Prize. His expository efforts have communicated the principles of economics to countless college and university students who have labored through his famous introductory textbook. And lately, he has been contributing a monthly column to *Newsweek*, keeping his textbook "alumni" thinking about economic issues and public policy. In a recent *Newsweek* essay on "Inequality,"[4] Samuelson reminded his readers that income and wealth are quite unevenly distributed in America. He noted approvingly that some superiority in income will always be around to reflect harder work and special needs. "But looking at

the matter in the abstract, some reduction in the degree
of unnecessary inequality will be regarded as a desirable goal by most ethical, religious and philosophical
value systems." Value systems suggest action. Something *ought* to be done, we say. But conservative ana-
lysts tell us that nothing can be done, certainly not by
governments, to reduce the inequality that will always
be with us. Radicals, on the other hand, say that something can be done but it would require the destruction
of our class-dominated, competitively based economic
society to do it. Samuelson claims membership in the
"middle group who think that improving minimum
standards of living for those at the bottom is a desirable
goal. And who think that a gradual reduction in inequality and expansion of equality of opportunity is
both desirable and feasible." But how? Not simply
through increases in the minimum wage. Not simply by
trade union victories in collective bargaining. Nor will
closing the loopholes in our progressive income- and
death-tax structure be enough to do it. Samuelson
notes, however, that those loopholes are not there by
divine decree. They can be changed. So can the tax
structure itself.

This brings me back again to thoughts about the
critical role of the American middle class. If the middle
class wants those loopholes closed and if it wants the
tax structure itself altered in the direction of relative
egalitarianism, this will happen. A movement toward
equality is a movement toward a larger middle class.
Numerically, there are far more potential entrants to
the middle class from the lower ranks of society than
from the higher. Barriers to entry are mounted against
the poor by the middle class itself. Some would say that
there is no organization in the American middle class;

it is fragmented. I now say that the middle class *is* organized while fragmented. The organizing principle is opposition to income redistribution in this country coupled with opposition to genuine equality of opportunity for blacks.

I fear that middle-aged, middle-income, middle-brow, middle-of-the-road Americans will earn for themselves in this century the epitaph found in T. S. Eliot's "The Rock":

And the wind shall say:
"Here were decent godless people:
Their only monument the asphalt road
And a thousand lost golf balls."

It is so discouraging to know that we can eliminate poverty in the United States, but we do not have the will to do it. Our unwillingness to work seriously for the reduction of poverty in foreign lands makes the picture darker still.

Out of this darkness some bizarre developments are emerging in America and around the world. In February 1974, the Symbionese Liberation Army, composed of a handful of radical revolutionaries, all Americans, communicated by tape-recorded messages with Randolph A. Hearst, the millionaire editor of the San Francisco *Examiner*. His daughter Patricia was kidnapped, the communique related, in retaliation for "crimes" her parents had committed against the "oppressed people of the world." Mr. Hearst was chairman of a "fascist media empire." His wife, a member of the University of California Board of Regents, was involved in lending money to corporations that profit from "robbery, oppression and genocide." To show proper "repentance," demanded the SLA, the Hearsts had to arrange to distribute, within the month, $70 worth of "top-quality" food to every Californian on welfare, social security or food stamps, every convict on probation or parole, and every disabled veteran in the state. The goal of the SLA: "to destroy . . . the capitalist state and all its value systems."[5] A subsequent tape-recorded message carried Patty Hearst's voice. Her whereabouts still unknown, she used rhetoric radical enough to convince her family that she had been brainwashed by the SLA. She called herself a "soldier in the people's army." She addressed her father as "Adolph," and called her parents "clowns," the "pig Hearsts."

In England, several months before the emergence of the SLA in California and the disappearance of Patricia Hearst, Dr. Bridget Rose Dugdale, age 33, stood in a British courtroom and screamed at her father, a wealthy Lloyd's insurance executive, "I love you, but I hate everything you stand for!" In that courtroom she was convicted of leading a gang that looted her father's home of paintings and silver worth $192,000. She received a two-year suspended sentence. Not many months later this Oxford-educated, London University Ph.D in economics was accused of taking part in the theft of 19 paintings worth more than $20 million, stolen from the Irish mansion of Sir Alfred Beit.

As an economist, Dr. Dugdale held top positions with Britain's Ministry of Overseas Development with United Nations agencies. She was one of the first women accepted as a member underwriter at Lloyd's of London. According to the Associated Press, "somewhere along the line Miss Dugdale met Walter Heaton, a cockney jailbird who had taken to leftist politics. She became his mistress and together they set up a 'social

clinic' in a rundown London shop to help the poor."
Mr. Heaton was one of those jailed for the burglary of
the Dugdale household. His economist friend, according to news accounts, "sneered" at her own suspended
sentence as "class justice" and told the sentencing
judge: "You have turned me from a recalcitrant intellectual into a freedom fighter. I don't know of any finer
title."[6]

Toward the end of the 1960's, riots broke out in
poor black ghettos of Los Angeles, Detroit, Rochester,
Baltimore, Washington, D.C. and other American
cities. At bottom these were gross, blunt, violent and
very costly ways of getting a message across to white
America. When the gap is wide, extreme measures are
taken to communicate.

The bizarre happenings associated with the names
of Patricia Hearst and Bridget Dugdale—isolated in-
cidents, symbolizing violent discontent with the maldistribution of wealth and income in our world—are signals to be read with care not only by bewildered parents
ensconced in "the system," but by all those middle
Americans who admit that "the system" could stand
improvement but should by all means be preserved. Improvement should begin without delay. Otherwise destructive protests and the tragic waste of young idealis-
tic lives will multiply.

Many in the Catholic community who are reading
these signals and wondering what to do have been well
versed in natural law ethics; they are quite familiar with
the concepts of right and obligation. I would like to
move these concepts forward a bit to include the notion
of an ethical relationship between need and care. There
is a familiar ethical relationship between a right and the
corresponding duties within a person who possesses that

right. Also familiar is the ethical obligation on the part of one person to respect the rights of another. I would suggest a refinement of this style of moral discourse to include the recognition that a genuine human need constitutes a genuine human right. A corresponding capacity to meet that need constitutes a moral obligation.

The need-care ethic requires of affluent Americans first an attitudinal change—compassion toward the poor. Indeed, "you can be kind to them whenever you wish." All of the social signals are telling us there can now be no postponement on this score. Second, the need-care ethic requires affluent America to move more willingly toward equality, toward improving the life chances of the poor. This means income redistribution. (Mugging is a gross, blunt and violent form of income redistribution. There must be a better way!) Again, there can be no postponement.

The reader will wonder where to begin. Begin from the only starting point you have—yourself. Achieve what only you, assisted by God's grace, can achieve in yourself—effective attitudinal change. Resolve to care, and properly assess your capacity to do so. Then identify the human and ecological needs that you can meet, however modest your potential contribution. As you start meeting these needs you will find yourself in a spare-and-share frame of mind. You will be moving toward stewardship, responding to an interim ethic that will engage you in an effort to reduce poverty, share resources, and protect the environment.

"If you liked the energy crisis," quipped an economic journalist, "you're going to love the food crisis!"

Food, unlike oil, is a renewable resource. But food production requires great amounts of non-renewable fossil fuels, chemicals and mineral fertilizers. These are becoming scarcer and more expensive. The shock of the 1973-74 fuel crisis will be followed in early 1975 by the shocking spectacle of famine in Asia on a scale larger than the 1974 famine in the sub-Sahara and parts of India. Per capita food production worldwide has been remarkably stable over the past twenty years. In affluent countries like the United States, preferences have shifted over the years to diets that are high in animal protein. This has caused an unprecedented increase in the demand for grain to feed cattle. As Americans eat more meat (we have doubled our beef consumption over the past 20 years), less grain is available to provide basic diets for the hungry of the world. Hence the resolution that emerged in New York City on May 20, 1974 at a meeting of the Board of Directors of Bread for the World (BFW), a new ecumenical, American, Christian organization dedicated to fighting world hunger. BFW urged American Christians to abstain from meat three days a week as a means of assisting poor nations faced with food shortages. The abstinence would have a spiritual and religious significance like any penitential act, but it would also have practical consequences of benefit to the poor and hungry. This was explained by Roman Catholic Bishop Thomas Gumberton of Detroit who is Vice President of the organization. He told the press that a reduction in meat-consumption by Americans could increase grain reserves throughout the world since so much grain is now used to prepare beef for the American dinner table. The increased reserves could help nations that are now fighting off starvation. Dr. Eugene Carson Blake, a Presbyterian who is President of BFW and who formerly served as General Secretary of the World Council of Churches, commented, "I think it's the first time we've ever tried to get American

Protestants interested in such an action as abstaining from meat—and I doubt if it would have been suggested if the Catholic Church had not changed its fasting rules."[7]

So the reader who wonders where to begin and what to do can literally begin at home with the menu and the grocery list. But it does no good for you to consume less, if there is no delivery and distribution system to get the food thus saved into the stomachs of the poor. The delivery and distribution network will not simply happen. It has to be forged in a political process. Participation in that process should be viewed as a serious responsibility in affluent America because hunger is evidence of a genuine human need, a need that constitutes a genuine human right. In America, we have the productive capacity to meet a very large portion of that need on a worldwide scale.

Membership in an organization (better, a movement) like Bread for the World is another way to demonstrate concern. BFW is a citizen's lobby; its members contact their congressmen and other government leaders from time to time on U.S. policy matters that vitally affect hungry people. BFW also encourages the formation of local groups that discuss poverty and hunger issues in the context of ecumenical worship services. (Further information is available from Bread for the World, 602 East Ninth Street, New York, N.Y. 10009.)

Another organization that has emerged to focus Christian thought and action on many of these same issues in the Center of Concern (3700 13th St., N.E., Washington, D.C., 20017). The Center's focus is "Toward a World That Is Human." Rev. William F. Ryan, a Canadian Jesuit and Harvard-trained economist, is executive director of the Center. Typical of his activities and the Center's interests was Fr. Ryan's participation on a network documentary on population and social development ("The People Problem," NBC-TV, June 9, 1974). Linking effective population control to advancing levels of social development, Fr. Ryan told the televiewers, "As long as a child in the United States uses between 30 and 60 times more of the world's resources than a child born in India, population targets will make sense to the poor only when they are accompanied by consumption targets for the rich." Appearing on the same program, Lutheran Pastor Arthur Simon, founding father and Acting Executive Director of Bread for the World, said: "Only when the insecurities of hunger and poverty are removed do people readily choose to have small families. To expect poor countries to solve their population problems primarily through family planning is to suggest a path that no society in history, least of all our own, has ever followed." The point, of course, is that couples in developing countries will freely limit the size of their families when real social development takes place, when improved life chances are available to their children. Parents will have fewer children when it is unlikely that their children are going to die at an early age.

Both the Center of Concern and Bread for the World send monthly newsletters to their members.

These and other movements in the Church are on the growing edge of a new awareness of a truth that is as old as the Church itself. "What is the use of loading (Christ's) table with cups of gold," asked St. John Chrysostom, "if he himself is perishing from hunger?"[8] For, as St. Augustine recognized in speaking of Christ, "This man is men, and men are this man; for many are one, since Christ is one."[9] This man is all men! His crucifixion goes on. And Chrysostom has Christ speak to us about the *then* of his cross and the *now* of his crucifixion in these words: "I fasted for you then, and I suffer hunger for you now; I was thirsty when I hung on the Cross, and I thirst still in the poor, in both ways to draw you to myself and to make you humane for your own salvation."[10]

Forgetting, perhaps, that "this man is men," we have too long refused to move toward the hungry, the poor, the oppressed who have been lifted up on a cross of suffering in our midst. And refusing to be thus drawn, we miss not only the opportunity to administer to this suffering man who is all suffering men, but we also delay our reconciliation with the Father in the poor, hungry and broken Christ.

By tolerating the presence of the poor with us always, we resist being drawn to Christ. We also resist becoming more humane and human, for Christ is the mediator of the new humanity. By refusing to be sparing in the use of material creation, we run the risk of violating our stewardship. And in our refusal to share with the poor, we jeopardize the salvation for which we really quest when we collect and cling to material possessions. By "letting go," we could free the poor and free ourselves as well.

NOTES

1. See *Jerome Biblical Commentary* (ed. by Raymond E. Brown, S.S. *et al.*), Vol. I, No. 10:5, p. 180, and No. 10:39, p. 194.
   2. *Ibid.*, Vol. II, No. 42:83, p. 53.

3. New York: Doubleday & Company, Inc., 1974; excerpted in the New Orleans *States-Item*, March 15, 1974, p. B-10.

4. December 17, 1973, p. 84.

5. *Newsweek*, Feb. 25, 1974, p. 20.

6. *Boston Evening Globe*, May 6, 1974, p. 10.

7. *National Catholic Reporter*, May 31, 1974, p. 3.

8. *Hom. in Matt. 88, 3* (P.G. 58:778).

9. *In Ps. 127, 14* (P.L. 37:1686).

10. *Hom. in Rom. 15, 6* (P.G. 60:547-48).